JAMES DICKEY

NEAL BOWERS

JAMES DICKEY

THE POET AS PITCHMAN

A LITERARY FRONTIERS EDITION
UNIVERSITY OF MISSOURI PRESS
COLUMBIA, 1985

Library of Congress Cataloging in Publication Data

Bowers, Neal, 1948–
   James Dickey, the poet as pitchman.

   Includes bibliographical references.
   1. Dickey, James. 2. Dickey, James—Biography—
Careers. 3. Authors, American—20th century—Biography.
4. Copy writers—United States—Biography. I. Title.
PS3554.I32Z57   1985   811'.54   84-21956
ISBN 0-8262-0459-7

Acknowledgments
   A summer research grant from the Science and Humanities Research
Institute of Iowa State University and partial released-time awarded by
the Iowa State English Department's Research Committee helped to move
this book toward completion. Special thanks go to Daniel Barrett for his
keen interest in the project. My wife, Nancy, deserves laurels and roses
for listening, editing, typing, and being there.
N.B.
Ames, Iowa
September 1984

FOR NANCY, BRIGHT WEATHER AND FLOWERS

CONTENTS

BOOKS BY JAMES DICKEY

POETRY

Into the Stone (1960)
Drowning with Others (1962)
Helmets (1964)
Two Poems of the Air (1964)
Buckdancer's Choice (1965)
Poems 1957–1967 (1967)
*The Eye-Beaters, Blood, Victory, Madness,
  Buckhead and Mercy* (1970)
The Zodiac (1976)
The Strength of Fields (1979)
Puella (1982)
The Central Motion: Poems 1968–1979 (1983)

PROSE

Deliverance (1970)
Jericho: The South Beheld (1974)
God's Images (1977)

CRITICISM

The Suspect in Poetry (1964)
Babel to Byzantium (1968)
Self-Interviews (1970)
Sorties (1971)
Night Hurdling (1983)

I. Introduction

Throughout his career, James Dickey has enjoyed an unusually high level of public exposure by transforming the normally quiet occupation of poet into a job with celebrity status. His face is recognizable not only from the photos on his book jackets but also from appearances on such television programs as "Bill Moyers' Journal" and William Buckley's "Firing Line." Moviegoers have seen him as the pudgy southern sheriff in the film version of *Deliverance*, and millions of citizens watching the televised festivities surrounding Jimmy Carter's 1977 inauguration saw Dickey step forward as an unofficial poet laureate to read "The Strength of Fields."

None of this attention was the product of happenstance, nor was any of it unwelcome. Instead, it was vigorously sought after by a poet who took his act on the road and eagerly received all resulting recognition. No poet in this century, with the possible exceptions of Dylan Thomas and Vachel Lindsay, has publicized himself and promoted his work more actively than has James Dickey. Predictably, his unabashed pleasure in the spotlight has prompted many people, especially some in academia, to label him an egotist and a fame pursuer; and Dickey *is* undeniably interested in his own reputation and in his place in contemporary poetry. But he also claims to be working for the good of poetry and all poets, a difficult point to dispute because Dickey, in gaining attention for himself, has also performed valuable public relations work for poetry in general. He has, whether selfishly or unselfishly, been a pitchman for poetry.

The level of Dickey's visibility and the extent of his advocacy for poetry are perfectly illustrated in a 1982 advertisement by the International Paper Company titled "How to Enjoy Poetry." The two-page spread, which appeared in a variety of national magazines and was subsequently offered by International Paper as an offprint and as a poster suitable for framing, features a denim-jacketed Dickey looking pensively out over a lake. Bordering his picture are comments by the poet intended to help the reader "approach poetry so it can bring a special pleasure and understanding to your life." The advice is given in Dickey's characteristic voice, vigorous and plain-spoken, even visceral, as he exhorts, "When you read, don't let the poet write down to you; read up to him. Reach for him from your gut out, and the heart and muscles will come into it, too." This may strike the reader accustomed to thinking of poetry as a delicate exchange between an anemic writer and a hypersensitive reader as pretty rugged stuff. And that is no doubt the intent, for the square-jawed Dickey in the photo, facing the sun and the wind off the lake, exudes ruggedness. Surely, here is a man who knows something of guts and muscles.

Other remarks in the ad destroy any impression that poetry is an exclusive or obscure occupation: "The beginning of your true encounter with poetry should be simple. It should bypass all classrooms, all textbooks, courses, examinations, and libraries and go straight to the things that make your own existence exist: to your body and nerves and blood and muscles." Dickey urges the reader to get in touch with the surrounding world: "A handful of gravel is a good place to start. So is an ice cube—what more mysterious and beautiful *interior* of something has there ever been?" The objective, according to the poet, is to look at the world and truly see it. Anything, from a rock to a leaf, is worthy of close viewing and can bring the viewer to a new appreciation of the world and his place in it.

Elsewhere in the ad, Dickey encourages the reader to try his hand at composing: "Writing poetry is a lot like a contest with yourself, and if you like sports and games and competitions of all kinds, you might like to try writing some. Why not?" Specifically, we are invited to explore the limerick, presumably because the form is relatively simple but probably also because limericks are usually tough and sassy. The idea is to lead us away from any preconception that poetry is overly complex and focuses only on the abstract. Moreover, we are told poetry is not an ethereal game but is akin to athletic competition—re-enter guts and muscles.

According to Dickey, if we follow his advice we will find ourselves seeing things we never would have noticed before and exclaiming in wonder and surprise: "Who'd'a thunk it?"—"*I* thunk it!" This is the poet's final attempt to win us over, to make all skeptics see that even a National Book Award winner knows colloquial expressions, that he is really one of us and can be trusted. It is Dickey's last ploy to convince us to give poetry a chance.

Overall, the ad is an engaging piece of writing, but exactly what is it selling? International Paper probably did not sponsor such an expensive spread out of purely aesthetic or educational motives. The company stood to gain goodwill, at least. Moreover, because International Paper manufactures the product on which poetry (not to mention other, more commercial writing) is printed, its gains may ultimately be more tangible. As understated advertising, this promotion for the International Paper Company stands as a model.

However, the ad is ostensibly selling something else— poetry—and poetry could not have a better salesman than James Dickey. As a former adman in New York and Atlanta from 1955 to 1961, Dickey knows about writing copy to properly market a product. He wrote successfully for Coca Cola and Lays Potato Chips, so it is easy for him to apply that talent to packaging poetry. The strategy he employs in "How to Enjoy Poetry" is exemplary. Directing his words at an audience that is likely to be intimidated by or indifferent to his product, Dickey contrives to change those attitudes. First, he speaks plainly, without becoming abstract or academic. Then he works to rebut the objections to poetry most likely found in an audience such as the one he is addressing by insisting on the importance of an individual participation in and response to poetry. The whole being must become engaged, not just the head but the gut and muscles, too. Understanding poetry, he implicitly asserts, is not a passive parlor game but an active, almost physical exchange into which the reader must wholly enter. Clearly, Dickey aims to break some stereotypes and to create an interest in his product by making potential consumers perceive it in a way they have never before seen it.

Also implied in Dickey's pitch and analysis of audience are his own attitudes toward poetry. Evident is the familiar mystical thrust found in many of his poems, the desire to start with the sun or with smaller things and wait for something to happen. Presumably, what will arrive is some kind of illumination, a clarity of vision that enables the viewer to see the connectedness of things. Present, too, is the familiar male persona, the one criticized as being too macho but the one in which Dickey takes special delight. He speaks of blood-and-gut responses, of how writing poetry is like a game or sport. This is all part of Dickey's pose, this attempt to charm the reader into drawing a little nearer to poetry by speaking like a simple boy from Georgia who understands the world better in terms of football or hunting.

Looked at pragmatically, Dickey's pitch is something more than an indirect ad for a paper company and an apologia for poetry; it is also excellent publicity for James Dickey, something the poet never avoids. In fact, Dickey's poetic talents are easily matched by his self-promotional skills, and the two areas of expertise merge in a way unique to Dickey. Surely, no other contemporary poet has been interviewed more, both in print and on television. And Dickey has carried his verbal exposure even further by publishing a collection of "self-interviews." Unblushing self-promotion is the standard for Dickey, whether talking to himself on tape or publishing excerpts from his personal journal. In the latter case (*Sorties*), Dickey's excruciatingly self-conscious remarks include, among other things, a self-exhortation to "go for the glory" and a lament that he is sick of his imitators.[1]

1. James Dickey, *Sorties* (Garden City, N.Y.: Doubleday, 1971), pp. 101 and 95. Cited hereafter as *Sorties* in text.

4

Poets are not necessarily introverted or shy, but neither are they noted for a Madison Avenue style. Most write privately, publish in literary journals, and hope for eventual recognition. Moreover, most regard composing and marketing poems as unrelated and, in some cases, incompatible acts. For Dickey, however, the energy that generates a poem fuels other activities as well, and the product becomes inseparable from its packaging and promotion. By logical extension, Dickey's claim that he "never [has] been able to disassociate the poem from the poet"[2] reveals that he is bound not only to the poem but to the packaging and promotion as well. While this may not make the public Dickey any more palatable for those who dislike his celebrity, it helps to explain the impetus behind his search for personal fame. To promote Dickey is to promote Dickey's poetry and to advance poetry and poets generally. Dickey seems to believe in such a chain of influence, at least in a purely intellectual way.

We find in Dickey one of those hybrids that blooms from time to time. As in William Carlos Williams and Dannie Abse, in whom physician and poet converge to produce superior poetry (and, arguably, more humane medical care), Dickey's skills as a commercial writer combine with his poetic interests to make him, if not a better poet, then the particular kind of poet he is. In a profession sometimes noted for its detachment from the everyday world, Dickey stands out as a writer not content to let the poem survive "in the valley of its making," but chooses to carry it out into the world, even into the corridors of the busy executives.[3]

During the years Dickey worked in the advertising business, he took a book of poetry to the office each day, carrying it or the manuscript of one of his own poems "as if it were a bomb" "through the acres of desks where typists typed five carbons of The Tony Bennett Record Promo-

---

2. James Dickey, *Self-Interviews* (Garden City, N.Y.: Doubleday, 1970), p. 24. Cited hereafter as *SI* in text.

3. W. H. Auden, "In Memory of W.B. Yeats," in *W. H. Auden: Collected Poems*, ed. Edward Mendelson (New York: Random House, 1976), p. 197.

tion."[4] His was a subversive act, taking what mattered most to him into a place where it mattered not at all. But when he left at day's end, with his poetry under his arm or tucked away in his briefcase, Dickey may not have been aware of intrusions in the other direction. If poetry can help, however privately, to humanize the business office, how might the office operate on poetry and, in Dickey's case, on the poet?

I want to answer that question by considering James Dickey as a poetic "pitchman," but I do not intend that term to be pejorative. In particular, I do not suggest that Dickey's motives for writing poetry were not artistic. However, the same abilities that made him such a successful young advertising executive contributed to his success as a poet. He understood that to get ahead in the marketplace the poet must know how to promote his product, and he combined the businessman's pragmatic view of the world with the artist's sensibility. Dickey knew, better than his contemporaries, how to sell the things he had to offer: himself, the poem, and (in his own view) God.

I have no ambition to prove a one-to-one relationship between Dickey's advertising career and his activities as a poet. To attempt such a proof would be especially foolish because Dickey himself has made it plain that writing copy and composing poems were not compatible activities. Still, the copywriter and the poet intersect in interesting ways. Both have a special facility with language and both believe in the power of words. But saying that Dickey was a poet because he was an advertising copywriter is just as inaccurate as saying that he went into advertising because he was a poet. In the end, no such causal relationship needs to be asserted. Dickey was and is both poet and pitchman, led into each role by his unique attributes and his individual personality. Consequently, I am examining here the different but related aspects of Dickey's talent, a talent broad enough to make him successful in two areas usually con-

4. James Dickey, *Night Hurdling* (Columbia, S.C.: Bruccoli Clark, 1983), p. 352. Cited hereafter as *Night* in text.

sidered completely unrelated. Though Dickey's ability as a pitchman might not have been so apparent had he never worked as an advertiser, it is finally the ability and not its manifestation in commercial offices that provides the focal point for this study.

II. Selling the Poet

From 1963 throughout the decade, Dickey devoted several months each year to what he called "barnstorming" for poetry, traveling from campus to campus to read his work in an exhausting tour of one-night stands more suited to a rock'n'roll band than to a poet. Thanks to Dylan Thomas, who loomed before Dickey as "the only predecessor,"[1] and in part to the Beats, whom Dickey largely disdained, the climate was right during those years for poetry readings. Poems had been taken off the page and given back to the voice, reinvested with a vitality lacking in the poetry of the academy, and large, appreciative audiences turned out for most readings.

Writers like Allen Ginsberg appealed to the counter-cultural interests of college students and attracted crowds eager to hear someone speak against the establishment. By comparison, Dickey's emergence as a prominent reader during this time is doubly interesting because he was not connected with the Beats, nor did he write topical poems. In fact, Dickey criticized the pre-eminent radical poet of the day, Ginsberg, referring to *Howl* in a 1957 review as "the skin of Rimbaud's *Une Saison en Enfer* thrown over the conventional maunderings of one type of American adolescent, who has discovered that machine civilization has no interest in his having read Blake" (*Babel*, p. 53).

Later, at the height of the Vietnam War protests, Dickey was criticized by Robert Bly for not joining the antiwar movement. Returning the favor, Dickey said, "Robert Bly has no talent at all, but he keeps writing for a pre-tested public, the literary anti-Vietnam public" (*SI*, p. 72). This remark, along with the negative assessment of Ginsberg, constitutes more than a petty attack on his contemporaries; it is a strong assertion of independence, of a deter-

1. James Dickey, *Babel to Byzantium: Poets & Poetry Now* (New York: Farrar, Straus, and Giroux, 1968), p. 251. Cited hereafter as *Babel* in text.

8

mination not to be swept up in any popular movement but to maintain the poet's "freedom to select his own subject by virtue of what moves him as a human being" (*SI*, p. 72). Dickey exercised the privilege with astonishing success.

While most of his contemporaries were experimenting with projective verse and making social and political statements in their poetry, Dickey was exploring the metrical possibilities of the anapest and looking for ways to write about "war, about love and sex, about athletics, about being a Southerner, about hunting and flying and canoeing, about the flight of birds and the movement of animals and the feeling of swimming in the presence of fish" (*Babel*, pp. 281-82). This list of subjects becomes more idiosyncratic as it progresses, but even the familiar topics cited first, the "universals" of war, love, and sex, were things Dickey was determined to write about in his own way.

While the premium he placed on individuality kept him apart from the rebels and radicals it also prevented his seeking membership among the academics and formalists. Despite his early interest in traditional metrics, Dickey was never tempted to become a versifier, and so he was able to criticize Ivor Winters, the prince of meticulous form, as vigorously as he attacked Ginsberg, citing "the poverty of Winters's emotional makeup" and calling his poetry "lifeless and life-destroying" (*Babel*, pp. 183 and 185). Looking for his own place to stand, Dickey was unwilling to give up the new freedom and vitality claimed for poetry by the Beats or to abandon traditional metrics entirely. Instead, he took what he felt he could use from both sides and insisted on making it his own.

It was in this posture that Dickey presented himself to the public. Taking to the road as neither rebel nor traditionalist but as James Dickey, with his own subjects and his own style, he embarked upon a decade of enormously successful readings. Secretly thinking of himself (with uncharacteristic humility) as "rather colorless and uninteresting," as a man who had "written poems for years because he liked to write them," he found himself caught up in "a kind of literary Vaudeville," in which "it is not only poetry that is involved: it is the poet as well" (*Babel,* p. 250). Simply reading the poems was not enough; he felt he had to give his audiences a performance, and so he acquired a guitar to play at post-reading parties, to do "the something idiosyncratic" that people expected and that he grew to expect of himself (*Babel,* p. 250). Emulating Dylan Thomas, he began to drink too much at his receptions and wished for "the courage to get drunk *before* the reading" (*Babel,* p. 251). These and other aspects of Dickey's gradual conversion from mere poet to poet-showman are described straightforwardly in a 1965 essay, "Barnstorming for Poetry," a frank account of the psychology behind a poet's public persona.

Those who heard Dickey read during the sixties know how complete a showman he became. For example, at Vanderbilt University in 1968, hundreds of people packed an auditorium, many standing against the walls and sitting on the floor below the stage, to hear the premier poet of the day. When Dickey finished, the crowd gave him a standing ovation, didn't want him to leave, and after several encores, mobbed the stage to shake his hand. As a former Vanderbilt student, he had a home court advantage; yet Dickey's readings elsewhere brought audiences to their feet. The impact was made not only by the poems and the way they were read but also by Dickey's comments before each one, and by the presence of the man himself. He involved the audience in the poetry by making them not simply auditors but participants.

Believing that poet and poem are inseparably bound, Dickey capitalized on that relationship at his readings, selling himself and his poems simultaneously. Although he criticized some of his more flamboyant contemporaries— Bly with his serape and Ginsberg with his mantra—saying, "if you can really write, you don't need to dress up funny" (*Sorties,* pp. 6-7), Dickey, too, dressed up. But his costume was more subtle and much more winning. Eschewing props and using only the tools available to any poet at the podium—his voice and personality—Dickey created an enormously attractive presence. His greatest ability was putting an audience at ease and making poetry accessible to everyone. This he accomplished partly through his rich Southern accent, which surprised many listeners, but mostly through his unpretentious manner, which blended well with the way he spoke. Those intimidated by poetry or uncertain of their ability to handle its complexities were instantly put at ease by the plainspoken man on the platform, who seemed to be saying that if he could write it anyone could understand it. The more self-assured members of the audience found Dickey's lack of pretention refreshing.

The chief characteristics of a Dickey reading during the sixties were casualness and an air of confidentiality. As he spoke about each poem, he also revealed interesting, and often not strictly relevant, details about himself: that he never ate breakfast and could get up and get going without it, even on a morning when he woke with a hangover, for example.[2] This kind of self-revelation may not have done much to elucidate a particular poem, but it created a receptive attitude in an audience. The personal anecdote and the off-the-cuff confession earned audience attention and made Dickey a popular reader.

Dickey was also noted for his willingness to talk about poems before reading them, commenting not only on their sources or contexts but often on their meanings as well. "Encounter in the Cage Country" is a poem changed forever by Dickey's comments. The location of the poem's zoo is unspecified; Dickey, though, in his preliminary remarks at readings, always located the poem in London and identified himself as the poem's speaker. The story, as Dickey used to tell it (and as he records it in *Self-Interviews*, pp. 168-69), is that he and his family were visiting London. The rest of the family wanted to go sightseeing, but Dickey decided to take a personal tour of the pubs rather than join in their expedition. After innumerable pints and much camaraderie, Dickey found himself considerably drunk in the middle of the London Zoo. Armed with this information, the reader sees new meaning in the speaker's green glasses:

2. Paul O'Neil, "The Unlikeliest Poet," *Life*, 22 July 1966, pp. 70–71.

they are worn, in part, to disguise his drunkenness. And the games played before the panther's cage, particularly the drawing of an imaginary gun, take on a different quality in the context of the speaker's condition.

These details may weaken the poem and cheapen its mystical qualities, but they make it accessible to an audience. After all, here is a real man in a real, and perhaps even familiar, situation. The anecdote itself is funny, but the poem is only partly humorous; and so by the time Dickey has read through to the end the audience might have stopped smiling and started thinking about the "green eyes" connection. They have been eased into the poem's more serious observations without knowing it.

Dickey took to the road with the enthusiasm of an evangelist or a traveling salesman. Few poets have shown as much stamina and drive as he manifested in the mid-sixties when he put together lengthy tours, often reading on successive nights in different cities. The traveling took its toll, but Dickey was rewarded with enthusiastic audiences; and he willingly paid the price of fatigue to get his poetry before as many people as possible. Had he been selling vacuum cleaners or encyclopedias for commission, he could not have worked harder. Poetry was his product, and though he received honoraria for his performances, the real payoff for Dickey was in publicity. By the strength and appeal of his personality, Dickey interested a far larger audience in his work than he could have gained through publication alone.

There are, of course, notable precedents for Dickey's approach to marketing his work. Dylan Thomas comes immediately to mind, but an even more interesting predecessor is that largely forgotten poet Vachel Lindsay, who achieved notoriety during his lifetime for his reading tours. What began for Lindsay on the streets of New York as a kind of experiment to see if he could sell or give away copies of one of his poems developed into a life-long determination to take his poetry to the people. Lindsay carried with him a pamphlet titled *Rhymes to be Traded for Bread* and once walked from Illinois to New Mexico, a feat no other poet has matched, no matter how long he claims to have been on the reading circuit.

Dickey, too, has displayed something of Lindsay's missionary zeal, traveling across country because it does "some good for my craft and the people who practice it with devotion" and because "it gets the word around about poetry" (*Night*, p. 273). Of course, it also publicizes James Dickey, just as Lindsay's peregrinations introduced him to the public. Dickey's readings of the sixties are still talked about on many college campuses, not always because the readings themselves were memorable but because Dickey did or said something startling or outrageous, sometimes socially objectionable, which left a permanent mark in the minds of those who witnessed it.

A typical Dickey episode took place after his 1968 Vanderbilt reading as admirers queued up to buy a copy of *Poems 1957-1967* and have it signed. A woman of about sixty handed her book to Dickey and responded shyly, when asked how she would like the book inscribed, that he should write whatever he wanted. Dickey then asked, "How about 'In fond memory of all those passionate nights we spent together'?" Predictably, the woman blushed, unable to retort. Dickey smiled, scribbled on the flyleaf, and returned the book to her. Whether he actually wrote what he suggested is unimportant; the significant thing is that in saying it he upheld the Dickey legend. Here was the hard-drinking, womanizing poet from whom even an elderly woman in an autograph line was not safe.

The Dickey persona, the one who traveled the reading circuit, stimulated interest in Dickey's poetry. He was, by reputation, an imposing figure, capable of being charming or insulting, depending on his mood and on how much he had drunk. Dickey's departure in 1956 from the faculty of the University of Florida after reading a poem called "The Father's Body" to a group of women added substantially to the Dickey legend. The women, mostly faculty wives, objected to what they felt were sexually explicit poems and demanded an apology via President J. Wayne Reitz. Refusing to apologize, Dickey resigned and left academia for the corridors of business in New York. Similar encounters with audiences objecting to the sexual nature of some of his poems, most notably "The Sheep Child," gave Dickey the reputation of a controversial poet, willing to take on taboo subjects even at the risk of shocking his audiences.

Dickey cultivated this reputation, because he found it was good for business. After all, a poet who may say something scandalous in a reading is far more alluring than one who offers his well-known set pieces every time. By today's standards, of course, a poem like "The Sheep Child" seems innocuous, but in the mid-1960s it was bold and promised even more risque material. And this possibility, an essential element of the Dickey persona, drew a great many people to his readings.

Just how conscious Dickey was of playing the bad boy is revealed in the following journal excerpt from *Sorties*:

> I think with terrible sadness of the evening spent with the astronauts a couple of nights before Walter Schirra's lift-off. I was drunk out of my mind, and could not focus on anything that happened, but simply sat in a corner in a drunken stupor attempting conversation with one or another nice young fellow who drifted by, doubtless out of a sense of duty, or of some kind of obscure loyalty to the *Life* people I was with. That opportunity will not come to me again, that is certain. And yet if I had been cold sober, what would I have done? Would I have been an eager-eyed middle-aged fellow, terribly receptive to all their personalities, and so on? No; if I had it to do again, I would be a drunken poet among the astronauts. And, by God I was a drunken poet. I remember them; now let them remember me. (*Sorties,* pp. 55-56)

What comes through most clearly in this recollection is an unrepentant tone. Dickey indulged in the role of Dionysian poet in the midst of the Apollo (that is, Apollonian) astronauts as though it were his duty to represent the reckless temperament in the presence of so much discipline and control. Such behavior gets noticed and contributes to the image of the poet as an irreverent, unpredictable character; and that is precisely the image Dickey cultivated.

Dickey's awareness of his public persona is sharply expressed in his following remarks on Byron: "He is the example of the kind of man that I've always attached a particular kind of personal value to. The guy who is an enormous phony, but who makes the public take him on his own terms, the terms of his persona. And underneath it all is an extremely practical, hard-headed, and utterly honest person" (*Night,* pp. 254-55). Dickey might well be describing himself in these remarks, for he, too, has offered the public a special version of himself, and that is the only James Dickey a great many people see: the swaggering former football player who stalks deer with a bow and hunts snakes with a homemade blowgun. The poetry suggests that there must be a more sensitive person behind all that machismo, but Dickey himself has done little to reveal his "practical, hard-headed, and utterly honest" self. Quite the contrary, he has promoted and gloried in his public persona, alienating some people in the process but always generating interest in himself and, by extension, in his work.

Although Dickey cites Byron as a model, there is something peculiarly American about Dickey's persona, something evoking the spirit of Whitman, that prototypal American poet. Whitman, too, shocked his readers, to expand the territory that could be considered poetic and to enlarge his readers' consciousness. He presented the public image of an unschooled eccentric; his poetry, however, betrays a man well read and enormously sensitive. Everything about Dickey—the casualness of his Southern dialect, the anecdotes he tells at readings, even the sports and hobbies he pursues and talks about—projects a good-old-boy image. As with Whitman, though, one finds a sizable intellect and considerable talent behind the facade.

Dickey also shares with Whitman a formidable ego, one that asserts not simply "I am important" but "I am artistically significant." This uniquely American bravado has cost both poets readers who value modesty. Whitman's work proclaims that he holds the torch and leads the way into the future. After Theodore Roethke—the poet Dickey most admired—died in 1963, when Dickey was asked to name the greatest living poet, he would respond, "James

Dickey." Probably most poets secretly regard themselves as the best, but few would publicly expound that view. With Dickey, the proclamation carries the conviction of an advertiser who sees nothing to gain by calling his product second or third best and so says it is *the* best. The claim itself then creates the reality. If superiority is proclaimed vigorously enough, people accept the claim as objective fact. The sales strategy that works for toothpaste and laundry soap also works for poetry; Dickey has demonstrated its efficacy.

The public Dickey persona is nowhere better revealed than in a 1966 *Life Magazine* article, "The Unlikeliest Poet." The title itself reflects the persona, suggesting that Dickey does not fit any stereotypes the reader may hold about poets. It also suggests, rather curiously, that some people are likely poets, implicitly reinforcing certain stereotypes. The only likely poet produced by America in this century is Robert Lowell, who had a genetic head start. The rest were descendants of railroad men and industrialists from such unlikely places as Hailey, Idaho, and St. Louis, Missouri. So Dickey is not such an aberration as the article title suggests. Still, his background does make interesting reading, especially because Dickey has taken such care to preserve and polish some of its ornaments.

Above the article's title, in smaller type, appears the following lead-in: "James Dickey—athlete, pilot, ad man and a fresh, emerging literary voice."[3] These are touch-points of a career that, ostensibly, should have led anywhere but to poetry, and they are exactly the things Dickey himself would have used to synopsize his life in an advertising logo. According to the article, "Dickey looks, acts and often talks exactly like a professional football coach; he stands 6' 3", weighs 205 pounds and, at 43, has the incipient paunch and huge biceps, the direct eye and the soft, half-humorous, half-challenging Southern voice which so often characterize those hulking ex-athletes who run teams in the National Football League."[4]

3. Ibid., p. 68.
4. Ibid.

This is precisely the image Dickey has cultivated, with obvious success. Everything is calculated to make the stranger, upon meeting Dickey for the first time, pause to think, "He certainly doesn't look or act like a poet." Exactly how a poet should look or act is open to conjecture, but the common stereotype is a ridiculous caricature: a much smaller, possibly consumptive fellow with an effete manner and a pedantic smirk on his face. Consequently, a considerable part of Dickey's self-marketing and of his public relations work for poetry in general was dedicated to the repackaging of the poet himself.

These considerations of physical size recall a remark made by Richard Hugo, himself a fairly large specimen. Hugo remembered being told by his teacher, Theodore Roethke—another poet big enough to have been mistaken for a football player—that the two of them presented a kind of presence to others because of their size, and as a consequence of the role dictated by their physical proportions felt a pressure that was fundamental to writing poems.[5] There is something almost primitive in this perception: the biggest and strongest member of the tribe has the duty to lead the others. In Roethke's case, though, the big man would lead through a landscape of images and ideas toward some spiritual goal rather than through a jungle of crouching beasts.

For Dickey, as for Roethke, physical stature is regarded as an asset; for Dickey, though, it is less a manifestation of some kind of poetic natural selection than an opportunity to disarm and engage an audience by contradicting its expectations of what a poet should look like. As Paul O'Neil put it in his *Life Magazine* article, "His very size comes as a surprise and he achieves an instant Strangler-Lewis-at-the-shoe-clerk's-convention command of audiences."[6] This preoccupation with size must be a liability in some ways, at least insofar as it is a male neurosis. Surely no woman poet has ever found herself saying, openly or implicitly, that she

5. Richard Hugo, *The Triggering Town* (New York: W. W. Norton, 1979), p. 34.
6. O'Neil, "The Unlikeliest Poet," p. 70.

17

is a poet because of or in spite of her size. It is regrettable that a man who finds himself becoming a poet feels it necessary to proclaim that he is a man for all that. Some have found Dickey's protestations extreme and even offensive, but he has used his claims of manliness to create a public persona that has elicited a more intense interest in both the poet and his poetry than might otherwise have been obtained.

A corollary to physical size is often athletic prowess, and so the *Life* article highlights Dickey's competitive skills, featuring photos of a young Dickey competing in the 120-yard high hurdles (in which he was Tennessee state champion) and carrying a football in a classic yearbook pose (as "a prize freshman back at Clemson").[7] But these activities seem mere adolescent rites of passage alongside Dickey's described participation in the Second World War as a pilot who flew approximately one hundred combat missions with the 418th Night Fighters in the Pacific, "sitting in a glass treasure-hole of blue light, / Having potential fire under the undeodorized arms / Of his wings, on thin bomb-shackles, / The 'tear-drop-shaped' 300-gallon drop-tanks / Filled with napalm and gasoline."[8]

This, then, was "the unlikeliest poet," at least in one writer's view in 1966: an athlete, a bomber pilot, a businessman successful enough in the advertising trade to be named Atlanta's "Young Man on the Go." And if these things did not make him unlikely enough, he was also a Southerner of unpretentious disposition who could provide an interviewer with eye-catching running headlines: "He likes people who moonshine and hunt."[9] Dickey has come to lament this kind of focus, wishing that people would "quit paying so much attention to me and to my interests—hunting and driving fast cars and that sort of thing" (*Night,* p. 272). But Dickey created the interest in his personal background and life-style, and though he has

7. Ibid., p. 68.
8. James Dickey, *Poems 1957-1967* (Middletown, Conn.: Wesleyan University Press, 1967), p. 181. Cited hereafter as *Poems* in text.
9. O'Neil, "The Unlikeliest Poet," p. 73.

perhaps grown tired of the attention his private activities receive, he is undoubtedly aware that much of that attention has spilled over to his poetry.

Almost any poet can be considered unlikely if one scrutinizes his background. A good many have, in fact, shared some of Dickey's "unlikely" experiences, though none has received quite the notoriety for them that Dickey has. Howard Nemerov was also a pilot in World War II and flew numerous fighter missions in the North Sea area. Richard Eberhart had military experience as a gunnery officer in the navy and was, for a while, an advertising copywriter in Chicago and later an assistant manager of the Butcher Polish Company. Theodore Roethke, while teaching composition at Penn State, coached the tennis team and was himself a ferocious competitor on the courts.

Such examples are easy to accumulate, and while they show that Dickey's background was less than unique for a poet, they also suggest that Dickey himself was responsible for calling certain aspects of his life to public attention. At the least, he did little to diminish the interest shown in his personal life. I draw this conclusion not to criticize Dickey but simply to point out how the poet was sold to the public. After all, Dickey, in calling attention to himself, was true to his philosophy that poet and poem are fundamentally inseparable. And he knew that some people in the crowd gathered to watch a flamboyant pitchman will buy what he is selling before they move on.

The public Dickey who became familiar to audiences across the country through readings was given a kind of solidity and permanence with the publication of *Self-Interviews* in 1970 and *Sorties* in 1971. Both books met with much negative criticism because they were "seemingly just too much of a self-congratulatory ego trip through Dickey's own memories and critical prejudices to be taken seriously as literary criticism." [10] They were, in many respects, a permanent recording, and in some cases a near transcription,

10. Richard J. Calhoun and Robert W. Hill, *James Dickey* (Boston: G. K. Hall, 1983), p. 130.

of things Dickey had said for years in interviews and at his readings. Many readers objected to the bodying forth of the Dickey public persona in all its self-absorption and immodesty. It was one thing to have a poet talk about himself in a reading but quite another to have him set down in print what passes for his most private ruminations. Admittedly, it is irritating to read a comment deliberately intended to shock—"The best abdominal exercise is fucking" (*Sorties*, p. 67)—and troubling to encounter the kind of self-pity and self-love reflected in the following passage:

> I am not what I seem to the world to be; a fine-looking fellow in the prime of life, big enough and strong enough to do almost anything he wants to do, a talented writer and the rest. No; I am a haunted artist like the others. I know what the monsters know, and shall know more, and more than any of them if I can survive myself for a little while longer. (*Sorties*, p. 73)

Such teary preening before the mirror goes down hard with most readers, who feel, despite the presentation of this passage as a journal entry, that affectations of this type are best left unrecorded.

Some critics have defended Dickey's forays into self-interviewing and journal publishing as a postmodernist critical stance and have claimed that Dickey is reacting against Eliot's concept of the transparent poet and the New Critics' notion of the intentional fallacy by bonding himself to his work and telling all.[11] In view of Dickey's claim that the poet and the work are "absolutely incapable of being disassociated from each other," this argument has merit (*SI*, p. 24). Dickey himself says, "I would agree with Malcolm Lowry, who read a Norwegian poet who wrote about the sea, Nordahl Grieg, and went to Norway just to meet him, because he had such strong feelings about coming together with the man who could have written those poems" (*SI*, p. 24). While the work may lead in this way to the poet,

11. Ibid., pp. 130–32.

the reverse is not necessarily true: the poet may not lead to the work.

Some risk is involved in using the poet as a lure to draw readers to the poetry. Dickey worked the connection to good advantage in his readings, at which poet and poem were indeed inseparable and were presented simultaneously to audiences. But the poetry has been almost entirely separated from the poet as he is presented in *Self-Interviews* and in the "Journal" section of *Sorties*. Consequently, the reader coming to the man first, at least as he is presented in those two books, may feel in no way led toward the poetry. Ironically, books intended to capitalize on the public's fascination with James Dickey, presumably in order to generate interest in his poetry, may in fact have diminished that interest.

When Dickey says in a reading that he gets started each morning without breakfast, even on the days when he is hungover, his remark produces laughter and provides a quick glimpse into the private life of the man at the podium. But when he writes, "I have been drunk, more or less, for about the last twenty-five years. Everything I remember is colored at least to some extent by alcohol" (*Sorties*, p. 84), the remark seems either an embarrassing confession or an adolescent boast. This is the problem with the entire "Journal" section of *Sorties*, which shows not so much the mind of the poet at work as the posturings of the ego. Even when the journal entries ring true, they are nearly always undercut by self-consciousness, as in Dickey's sad reflections on his relationship with Robin Jarecki, when she was twenty-nine and he was forty-three. Dickey is careful to note that he learned of her untimely death as he sat at his "official desk at the Library of Congress," and he concludes his melancholy remarks by slipping into German and then translating himself: "*Es muss sein. Es muss sein.* It must be. It must be" (*Sorties*, pp. 70-71). This has the flavor of something written to be read, not written just to record a fleeting personal thought or reverie, as true journal entries are. Similarly, Dickey's prescription for dealing with not winning the Nobel Prize and his lament that he is sick of his imitators are things put down for the consumption of others, not for the private expression of self (*Sorties*, pp. 104 and 95).

Although *Self-Interviews* and *Sorties* were logical products of Dickey's ongoing attempts to sell his poetry by selling himself, those books contributed to a significant devaluation of his work. As long as Dickey was barnstorming the country and talking about himself and his poetry at the same time, he was a character of legendary proportions. But when he began talking about himself at length in print he created a distance between the poet and his poetry that led many people to disdain the one and ignore the other. It is no mere coincidence that *Self-Interviews* and *Sorties* stand at the end of a decade during which Dickey made his phenomenal rise to prominence and at the beginning of a decade in which he and his poetry were largely neglected. They represent the point of saturation, the point at which the market could bear no more of Dickey's principal commodity, himself. Moreover, they created a backlash that still keeps many readers from fully appreciating the poetry.

Also marking the transition between decades and contributing to the diminishment of interest in Dickey's poetry was his first, and so far only, published novel. Although Dickey himself has insisted that "the least poem I've ever written is better than the whole of *Deliverance*" (*Night*, p. 196), he is known to many readers only as a novelist, thanks to the success of his single venture into fiction. As Dickey has put it, "If you write a novel that's successful, and made into a movie, it gives your enemies a weapon against your poetry; that is, they say, 'You should have been writing novels.' They use the novel to beat the poetry with" (*Night*, p. 196).

Predictably, when *Deliverance* was published, many readers and reviewers did just the opposite, used the poetry to put down the novel, labeling Dickey's effort an amateurish foray into unfamiliar territory. But the novel met with considerable popular success, was helped along by the film version, and proved to have considerable staying power. This has led to an interesting reassessment and, in what earlier reviewers labeled merely an entertaining adventure story, later critics have found profuse archetypal and mythological significance and have seen parallels between *Deliverance* and a diverse group of novels, including *The Deerslayer*, *Huckleberry Finn*, and even *Heart of Darkness*. If the initial reviewers of Dickey's novel erred by not taking it seriously enough, subsequent readers have perhaps committed the opposite offense by taking it too seriously. I am reminded of Dickey's remark about contemporary poetry criticism: "Far too much is made of far too little" (*Sorties*, p. 6). Not that the novel lacks substance. To be sure, it is more than a diverting tale of the outdoors, but it is not *Heart of Darkness* despite its potentially symbolic river and its thematic preoccupation with the primitive instincts vestigial in even suburban man.

One of the most revealing observations about *Deliverance* is Dickey's claim that he knew from the beginning the novel would be "a winner" (*Sorties*, p. 102). Whatever else that term may imply, it undoubtedly means that Dickey wrote *Deliverance* because he felt it would be a popular success. Many would-be novelists have felt the same, but few have had the luck or skill to gauge the public's interest so accurately. Dickey's story of four businessmen struggling with nature, their fellow man, and the darker sides of themselves found an eager audience in 1970.

The survivalist instinct that manifested itself in the shape of backyard bomb shelters in 1962, when Dickey began writing *Deliverance*, had become a more specific notion of self-sufficiency by the latter part of the decade and found perfect expression in the characters of Lewis Medlock and his friend Ed Gentry. Playing on a basic distrust of technology and fear of what the world might be like in the aftermath of a nuclear war in which cities were destroyed, the novel asks a single, fundamental question: If the machines should fail and suburban man should find himself in a primitive condition in the wilderness, could he survive? The novel itself answers this question affirmatively in the character of Ed Gentry.

Like any good novelist, Dickey put a good bit of himself into his fiction. The canoeing, hunting, archery, and the emphasis on physical fitness are all central to him personally. But while all four principal characters represent aspects of Dickey's personality, Lewis Medlock and Ed Gentry afford special insight into the Dickey persona, and the novel is essentially a mediation between these two characters. Ed, the adman whose life has grown stale, must discover that he can do more than he ever imagined possible; while Lewis, the self-assured fitness buff and outdoorsman, must come to terms with his own limitations. By the end of the novel, each has had his self-concept and world view modified sufficiently enough that common ground is attained, and Ed and Lewis share a single perception. Because Dickey is both men, both adman and outdoorsman, the novel shows the reassembling of the personality Dickey divided to create his two most important characters in the first place.

Not surprisingly, then, if Dickey is both Ed and Lewis simultaneously, the merging of these two personalities in the novel forms an artistic temperament and leads to the production of art. As Ed reflects near the end of the narrative, "The river underlies, in one way or another, everything I do. It is always finding a way to serve me, from my archery to some of my recent ads and to the new collages I have been attempting for my friends."[12] Ed even rehires George Holley, the "serious" artist he had earlier fired, and talks at length with him about art. The reinstatement of Holley, who always seemed to be saying "I am with you but not of you" (*Deliverance,* p. 15), shows clearly that Ed has won back at least some of the artistic sensitivity he had lost to the commercial world. As with the mixture of adman and woodsman in Dickey, the convergence of Lewis Medlock and Ed Gentry, incomplete in themselves, leads to the creation of a fuller personality, one capable of artistic expression. Dickey is saying that the artist is the man in touch with all aspects of himself, even with his more primi-

12. James Dickey, *Deliverance* (Boston: Houghton Mifflin, 1970), pp. 275-76. Cited hereafter as *Deliverance* in text.

tive side, and the novel becomes an implicit explanation and justification of the multifaceted Dickey personality.

Reading *Deliverance* as Dickey's *apologia pro vita sua* may seem to restrict the novel within too narrow a range of meaning. But it is a reading, an approach to the novel, that has been overlooked. *Deliverance*, regardless of what else it may do, comments on art and on what Dickey has called "the energized man," the man who has come to see the world in all its variety and beauty and mystery and asks, "'Why are men content to go through life with so little recompense? Why will they not make just a *small* effort? Why must they be content to have, really, so little of themselves?'"[13] To Dickey's mind, the ultimate horror is "to pass on without having had more than a fraction of one's own life—own interests, own perceptions, own sense of consequence."[14] It is the poet, as energized man, who stands against this meaninglessness and aimlessness. Dickey, in his own life, has struggled to stand with the poet. And it is Ed Gentry's good fortune to take his place alongside them, having been energized by his experience on the Cahulawassee.

Deliverance can best be understood in relation to *Self-Interviews*, published in the same year, and *Sorties*, which came out a year later. All three books offer special views of James Dickey. One is a fictional presentation of Dickey's world view and perhaps even a vindication of his life-style; another is a monologue transcribed from tape, rich in autobiographical detail; and the third comprises the journal revelations of what pass for a man's most private thoughts. Together, the three present a multidimensional view of James Dickey, and they even comment on one another in interesting ways, as when Dickey says in an entry in *Sorties*, "I am Lewis; every word is true" (*Sorties*, p. 75).

This claim enhances the reader's interest in *Deliverance* by piquing his curiosity and making him wonder if that

13. James Dickey, "The Energized Man," in *The Imagination as Glory: The Poetry of James Dickey*, ed. Bruce Weigl and T. R. Hummer (Urbana: University of Illinois Press, 1984), p. 165.
14. Ibid.

III. Selling the Poem

No one in this century has talked and written more about his poetry and his poetics than has James Dickey. In this respect, he has been the ultimate pitchman. The fear that saying too much about the creative process might somehow weaken or destroy it, an abiding neurosis of many contemporary poets, appears not to bother Dickey. In fact, he seems to fuel his creative drive by responding at length to questions put to him, no matter how trivial they may sound or how repetitive they may have become over the years. Consequently, we know a great deal about how Dickey works and what he hopes to accomplish in his poetry. We have, for example, his claim that he writes all the time, even in his sleep, and that he considers himself "one of those slow, plodding, searching writers" (*SI*, p. 63). We know that he revises laboriously and always has three or four different things in progress simultaneously, in different typewriters scattered around his house.

Dickey talks about these things because they are mysterious and interesting to him. Like the man who can move small objects without touching them and without knowing how he does it, Dickey is as intrigued by his own creative powers as outside observers are. All his talk reflects a person trying to understand the poetic process himself, not a writer who has reduced everything to convenient formulas. This attitude explains in part why Dickey would be interested in interviewing himself or in telling everything he knows about the origin and writing of a poem. Beyond the obvious and much criticized jungle of egocentrism lies a surprisingly large lake of objectivity and simple curiosity.

The problem for the reader wishing to follow Dickey's self-analysis is basically one of abundance. There is so much material that it is difficult to know where to begin. Luckily, Dickey is remarkably consistent in his poetic philosophy, even to the point of being repetitive, and that helps to make things more manageable. Of particular interest to this study is a remark Dickey made about his earliest poetry, one he has stood by through all the changes in his subsequent work: "I wanted immediacy, the effect of spontaneity, and reader involvement more than anything else. I also wanted to see if I could work with narrative elements in new and maybe peculiar ways" (*SI*, p. 47). If an entire career can be summarized in such a small space, these two statements tell the whole story of his poetic endeavor: the desire for reader involvement and the attempts to effect it through narrative experimentation.

At a Dickey reading, there has never been any question that the audience would become involved in the performance of the poetry, thanks largely to Dickey's engaging presence. But Dickey is talking here about participation for the reader rather than the auditor. Borrowing a term from Alfred North Whitehead, Dickey says that he is after "presentational immediacy," but not in an oral sense:

> No, I don't mean the presentation, say, from a reading platform. I mean, for words to come together into some kind of magical conjunction that will make the reader enter into a real experience of his own—*not* the poet's. I don't really believe what literary critics have believed from the beginning of time: that poetry is an attempt of the poet to create or recreate his own experience and to pass it on. I don't believe in that. I believe it's an awakening of the sensibilities of someone else, the stranger. (*Night*, p. 302)

These observations about the reader and his relationship to the created work clearly place Dickey with the phenomenologists. He is more interested in the affective possibilities of his poetry and in the reader's ability to respond to that poetry in an individual and private way than in handing over a parcel containing his own attitudes and emotions. According to Dickey, the poetic exchange ought to produce "an awakening of the sensibility of someone else. It's giving *his* experience to *him*. It's revitalizing his experience, rather than trying to pass yours on to him" (*Night*, p. 302).

It is not clear whether Dickey would go so far as to say

the work itself is secondary to the reader's response, existing only in the reader's consciousness. He approaches analysis of his own poetry with the eye of a New Critic, saying all the while, "I'm not trying to impose an official interpretation on the poems; that would be the last thing I would want to do. As one reader of my verse and as the person who happened to create the poems, I offer the following remarks for whatever interest they have to people who want to look at the poems from my standpoint as well as their own" (*SI*, p. 83). Significantly, Dickey regards himself as "one reader" of his poetry among many probable readers, all presumably capable of responding in their own ways, regardless of what Dickey may have to say. But unlike the true New Critic, who would disallow the poet's comments on his own work on the grounds of the intentional fallacy, Dickey insists on his right to be affected by what he has written and to talk about how he as a reader receives the poems.

If "presentational immediacy" is the objective, narrative is the technique Dickey employs to attain it. Curiously, though, some critics have failed to acknowledge Dickey as a narrative poet. Paul Ramsey, for example, has identified Dickey as a failed lyric poet, saying, "a great lyric rhythm found him; he varied it, loosened it, then left it, to try an inferior form."[1] In reality, a very different process occurred: Dickey had a brief, early flirtation with the lyric, during which time he was embarrassingly derivative, but he soon discovered his true power and originality in the narrative, which, as a staple of English and American poetry, is far from being an inferior form. To see just how unformed Dickey was as a lyric poet, one needs only to look at some passages from his first book, *Into the Stone* (1960). There we find echoes of Dylan Thomas:

> Nor rise, nor shine, nor live
> With any but the slant, green, mummied light

1. Paul Ramsey, "James Dickey: Meter and Structure," in *James Dickey: The Expansive Imagination*, ed. Richard J. Calhoun (Deland, Fla.: Everett/Edwards, 1973), p. 177.

And wintry, bell-swung undergloom of waters
                                        (*Poems*, p. 24)

the voice of Hopkins made thin through anapests:

> Now, owing my arms to the dead
> Tree, and the leaf-loosing, mortal wood,
> Still hearing that music amaze me,
> I walk through the time-stricken forest
>   (*Poems*, p. 35)

and Roethke unabashedly cribbed:

> The dead have their chance in my body.
> The stars are drawn into their myths.
> I bear nothing but moonlight upon me.
> I am known; I know my love.
>   (*Poems*, p. 48)

The most memorable poem in that first volume is "The Performance," and it is not merely coincidental that the poem is a strong narrative. For Dickey, finding his own true voice coincided with discovering the narrative and working less with the lyric. What he wanted was the poetry of participation rather than of reflection, and he found it and the possibility for increased reader involvement in the narrative (*Sorties*, p. 59).

This, then, is how Dickey sells the poem, by using narrative techniques and involving the reader in some kind of action. In Dickey's own words, he "wants, more than anything else, for the poem to be an experience—that is, a *physical* experience—for the reader. It must be a completed action, and the plunging in of the reader into this action is the most difficult and the most desirable feat that the poet can perform" (*Sorties*, p. 59). To achieve the effects Dickey wants most, the reader must be pulled into a dramatic situation. The lyric confronts the reader with reflection, but the narrative tells a story and beckons the reader to become involved with the action of that story. In this respect, Dickey has said that his work "attempts to win back for poetry some of the territory that poetry has unnecessarily relinquished to the novel" (*Sorties*, p. 58).

Having taken the position that he wanted for "most of [his] poems . . . a sense of *story*" (*Sorties*, p. 49), Dickey soon discovered great flexibility in the narrative form. Perhaps he oversimplified things in identifying only two basic ways to present a story: "One way is for the story to be obvious; that is, for there to be a beginning, middle, and end in that order. The other way is for the story to be implicit, and there are a million ways of doing this" (*Sorties*, p. 49). But even such a generalization shows how much potential he saw in the story poem. The poetry itself reveals a growing fascination with style and diction and their connection to point of view. The range reaches all the way from a standard narrative like "The Performance," to the first-person delivery of a sermon by a woman preacher, to the third-person accounts of what an airline stewardess's fall from an airplane might have been like and what a drunken, half-crazy Dutch poet determined to fix his position in the universe might think and say, to a woman's girlhood "male-imagined."

Dickey's growing interest in the narrative poem coincided with his starting to work on *Deliverance* in 1962. But if the novel in progress influenced his poetry, his poetry impacted on the novel, so much so that Dickey's final revisions of *Deliverance* were undertaken to stress "a straightforward novel more and the poetic aspects of a lyrical novel less."[2] The struggle to find some point of balance between lyric and narrative is central to Dickey's work, and though he has remained committed to the lyric, his poems succeed in almost direct proportion to their narrative content. That is why *Puella* (1982) disappoints: the narrative has been subordinated to the lyric.

The effort to reconcile narrative and lyric is clearly evident in several poems in Dickey's first book, *Into the Stone* (1960) but nowhere more so than in "Sleeping Out at Easter," which opens with this stanza:

2. Richard J. Calhoun and Robert W. Hill, *James Dickey* (Boston: G. K. Hall, 1983), p. 110.

> All dark is now no more.
> This forest is drawing a light.
> All Presences change into trees.
> One eye opens slowly without me.
> My sight is the same as the sun's,
> For this is the grave of the king,
> Where the earth turns, waking a choir.
> > *All dark is now no more.*
> > (*Poems*, p. 17)

In his comments on this poem, Dickey has said that he told himself before writing it to "Make it immediate. Put the reader and yourself *in medias res*, in the middle of an action" (*SI*, p. 86). The emphasis is on the narrative, as Dickey's use of the term *in medias res*, which describes the conventional opening of an epic poem, suggests. So we begin by waking somewhere with the speaker, apparently outside among trees. The title, of course, has already tipped us off to this; but still, the narrative engages us in a process of discovery as we come to see a man waking at dawn in his own back yard after a night of sleeping out. His wife, beginning to stir inside the house, sees him through a window; his child sleeps on, mystically feeling the significance of this situation.

Dickey himself sees two things in this poem. First, there is the story, which is "just about a man sleeping in back of his house and becoming another person on Easter through the twin influences of the Easter ritual and of nature itself. His rebirth is symbolized by nothing more or less than waking up in a strange place which is near a familiar place" (*SI*, p. 86). So much for the narrative component.

But Dickey also sees something mysterious in the poem, something that goes beyond the simple telling of a story, and that quality is communicated through lines with a "marked rhythmical effect," "an almost hypnotic beat" (*SI*, p. 86). This is the purely lyrical aspect of the poem, which is represented best by the final stanza, a combination of lines taken from throughout the poem and offered as a kind of coda:

32

> *All dark is now no more.*
> *In your palm is the secret of waking.*
> *Put down those seeds in your hand;*
> *All Presences change into trees.*
> *A feather shall drift from the pine-top.*
> *The sun shall have told you this song,*
> *For this is the grave of the king;*
> *For the king's grave turns you to light.*
> (*Poems*, p. 18)

Gathered as they are at the end, and italicized to suggest a greater significance, these lines stand as a lyrical comment on the narrative aspect of the poem. It is curious that Dickey felt, at least at this early point in his career, that the narrative could not carry the theme and suggest something of mystery on its own. Though it may be an interesting experiment, the poem has a heavy-handedness that keeps it from working as well as Dickey wanted it to. However caught up in the immediacy of the narrative readers might be, they are likely to lose interest by the end of the poem, when the narrator is pushed aside by the intrusive poet intent on resonating something mysterious.

By way of contrast, "The Performance" shows where Dickey's true powers lie, in a forceful narrative presentation. The immediacy Dickey hoped for in "Sleeping Out at Easter" is fully realized here, as the reader is swept up by the narrative voice from the very first statement:

> The last time I saw Donald Armstrong
> He was staggering oddly off into the sun,
> Going down, of the Philippine Islands.
> (*Poems*, p. 30)

Using a traditional narrative opening, which begins at the beginning rather than in the middle of things, Dickey's narrator immediately engages the reader with an evocative recollection of someone named Donald Armstrong. The locale, the Philippines, the simple assertion that this is a memory of seeing Armstrong for the last time, the ambiguous possibilities of the word "staggering," and the symbolic potential of Armstrong's movement into the setting sun all help to create an intriguing dramatic situation that draws the reader into the poem to discover more. What the reader learns is that Armstrong was in the Philippines during the war, that he was staggering because he was walking on his hands, and that he was killed by his Japanese captors the day after the speaker saw him looming precariously upside-down in the sunset.

Though it is arguable that "The Performance" is more interesting than "Sleeping Out at Easter" simply because of its subject matter, the effectiveness of each poem is largely determined by how its content is presented. While the speaker of "Sleeping Out at Easter" talks or thinks to himself in short sentences and end-stopped lines, the voice in "The Performance" directly addresses the reader in a more natural, conversational way. Accounting for this difference by saying it reflects the difference between lyric and narrative poetry may be tempting, but it does not accurately explain what distinguishes these two poems from one another. After all, "Sleeping Out at Easter" is a narrative, even though it resolves itself into pure lyric at the end; and "The Performance" certainly contains lyrical passages, such as the following:

> Standing there on his hands,
> On his spindle-shanked forearms balanced,
> Unbalanced, with his big feet looming and waving
> In the great, untrustworthy air
> He flew in each night, when it darkened.
>
> (*Poems*, p. 30)

This passage more than holds its own alongside "My child, mouth open, still sleeping, / Hears the song in the egg of a bird" (*Poems*, p. 18), the statement in "Sleeping Out at Easter" that Dickey finds filled with such resonance and mystery. What finally separates these two poems and makes them so different is Dickey's attitude. In the Easter poem, he strains after significance and ends by imposing mystery and meaning on the situation. But in remembering Donald Armstrong, he simply tells the story and lets the details body forth whatever significance they may have.

Dickey's attitude, or his poetic stance, impinges upon everything he has written and accounts for how the poet who could write a moving, troubling poem like "The Fire-bombing" could also write "The Poisoned Man" with its excess allegorical baggage. When Dickey trusts in his material and in his ability to order detail in the most evocative way, he is an exceptional poet. But when he gives his material a booster injection of meaning and significance he can be as tedious as Robert Service or as didactic as Edgar Guest. In his drive to find what he calls the "glory," Dickey has always been drawn to the lyrical, to the magical, incantatory qualities inherent in language. In fact, Dickey's more recent poetry (such as that in *Puella*) reveals an almost total commitment to the lyrical. This is a lamentable but perhaps inevitable defection from the narrative camp, the result of a career-long struggle to accommodate a lyrical impulse within the scope of a narrative gift.

It was Dickey's narrative poetry, however, that accounted in large part for his popularity during the 1960s, for his success in "selling" his work. Within the narrative poem, Dickey discovered a range of rhetorical strategies associated with the speaker's voice: repetition, mixed diction (formal with colloquial), and a complex sentence structure that allows the poem to gather speed and pull the reader along toward the syntactical and thematic climax. These techniques disarm, perhaps even mesmerize, and involve the reader as much as possible in the poem. Just as Dickey's voice and manner at the podium captured an audience, the voices speaking from the printed page invite the reader to participate fully in the poem. They may take on the tone of friend, confessor, carnival barker, or evangelical preacher, but all are designed to sell the poem by catching the reader up in it.

"The Performance" exemplifies Dickey's early efforts in what he called "mythologizing my own factual experience" (*SI*, p. 85). Extrapolating from the actual capture and decapitation of a fellow pilot named Donald Armstrong, Dickey imagines what his friend might have done before the sword fell. Because "you can make anything you like happen in a poem," he has Armstrong perform his acrobatics before kneeling down to be beheaded (*SI*, p. 94). The true potential of the subject matter is realized in the poem through what Dickey calls "the creative possibilities of the lie" (*SI*, p. 32). In Dickey's view, the poet "comes to understand that he is not after the 'truth' at all but something that he considers better. He understands that he is not trying to tell the truth but to *make* it, so that the vision of the poem will impose itself on the reader as more memorable and value-laden than the actuality it is taken from" (*Sorties*, p. 156). Of course, this kind of fabricating is the heart of fiction, and as an element essential to Dickey's poetic narratives it represents another way in which the reader's attention can be gained and held.

The only serious problem with pursuit of a truth better than truth is that it sometimes tends toward abstraction, as in the title poem of *Into the Stone*. Even if Dickey had not said so, we would have no trouble guessing that the poem has no factual context but is based instead on "a vague idea about the quality of a love relationship, especially in its early stages when it changes the world for the person in love" (*SI*, p. 98). Here, as in "Sleeping Out at Easter," Dickey is lured by the lyric as by the Siren's call, and he ends up on the rocks rather than moving "into the stone." The title itself reflects the terribly abstract nature of the poem, especially since Dickey never makes it clear what the stone might be or how it is possible to move into it. For help with such puzzles we have only the line "Through the stone held in air by my heartbeat" (*Poems*, p. 47). Whatever lyrical qualities this line may possess are more than offset by its obscurity. But here, as in "Sleeping Out at Easter," Dickey is principally interested in the mysterious qualities he can evoke through language. The lines are mostly end-stopped; the rhythm is either hypnotic (as Dickey would have it) or monotonous; and the man and woman are incorporeal. Had Dickey written only poems of this type, his books would never have been dog-eared and few people would have turned out to hear him read, even on a mild night in spring.

"The Lifeguard" is another poem that begins in the middle of things; unlike "Into the Stone," however, it offers a real character instead of a wispy shape in the moonlight. The speaker finds himself in the most human of situations, wishing to undo a tragic occurrence. When the poem opens, we find him in a boathouse at night, "From all sleeping children hidden" (*Poems*, p. 51). The dramatic situation created by this setting leads to speculation about the identity of the speaker and why he is hiding from the children. As curiosity draws us further into the poem, the speaker does something impossible:

> I rise and go out through the boats.
> I set my broad sole upon silver,
> On the skin of the sky, on the moonlight,
> Stepping outward from earth onto water
> In quest of the miracle
>
> This village of children believed
> That I could perform as I dived
> For one who had sunk from my sight.
> I saw his cropped haircut go under.
> I leapt, and my steep body flashed
> Once, in the sun.

(Poems, p. 51)

He is either walking on water or imagining himself to be, but however we read the poem we find ourselves, by this point, involved in an extraordinary narrative. The mood is not quasi-mystical, as in "Sleeping Out at Easter," or abstract-ethereal as in "Into the Stone," but true beyond the possibility of truth. Confronted with the implacability and the irreversibility of death, the lifeguard can only fantasize or actually perform a miracle. Nothing less will do. To save a child who is beyond saving, he must become Christ-like and resurrect him from the moon-illuminated lake.

The poem, then, represents the psychological stages in coming to terms with grief and, in this case, its attendant guilt. Having failed in his duty to protect the children swimming at the summer camp, the lifeguard withdraws from reality. His initial impulse is to hide from the truth and from his failure to save the drowning child. The second stage is to wish for the power to undo the death, and so he imagines himself walking across the lake to reclaim the lost boy. Both tactics, evasion and hallucination, finally give way to a confrontation of reality and an acceptance of the situation as the lifeguard washes the mud from his hands, symbolically absolving himself of guilt, having done all he could humanly do. He then turns his attention from himself to the child, for whom he is finally able to grieve.

Though "The Lifeguard" is not based on autobiographical fact, as is "The Performance," it is equally true. The specific character and the dramatic situation enable Dickey, or perhaps empower him, to create truth; and the poem succeeds to the extent that he is able to project himself into the character of the lifeguard and experience his predicament. The process of assuming a persona is central to what Dickey calls the fiction of the poem and involves answering some fundamental questions:

> The questions he must answer in this respect come to the poet in forms not so much like "What did I do then?" but rather "What might I have done?" or "What would it be interesting for me to do, given the situation as I am giving it?" Or perhaps, if the poet is prone to speak in this way, "What can I make my agent do that will truly *find* the poem: that will focus it on or around a human action and deliver a sense of finality and consequence, and maybe even that aura of strangeness that Bacon said every 'excellent beauty' must possess?" (*Sorties*, p. 157)

In other words, the poet does not discover a character and then search for things he might already have done. Instead, the poet and his character mutually inhabit one another and together create the facts of the poem. The process for Dickey involves vigorously pushing at the limits of credibility to make the persona do something truly memorable and, with luck, to discover "that aura of strangeness."

Even the casual reader of Dickey's poetry immediately

38

recognizes the quality of strangeness Dickey values so greatly. It is there in the brightening yard of a man sleeping outside at Easter, in the joyous, perfect acrobatics of a soldier about to be executed, and in the lifeguard's first step "from earth onto water." This fascination with the eerie, the bizarre, and even the grotesque is a hallmark of Dickey's work and has been one of the reasons for its appeal. One is not likely to encounter in the work of any other poet a sheep child speaking from a bottle of alcohol, an airline stewardess disrobing as she falls to her death, or a railroad bum becoming a celebrity after being nailed to the side of a boxcar. So strong is Dickey's attraction to the unusual that his poetry often tends toward surrealism, though it usually maintains touch, however tenuously, with reality. According to Dickey, "The poem should come of reality and go back into it. But it should *impose* itself on fact" (*Sorties*, p. 98). Certainly, that is what happens in "The Lifeguard," as we move from the speaker's attempt to hide, through his fantasy of resurrecting the drowned child, and finally to his acceptance of grief.

In great part, Dickey's popularity has been the product of his willingness (at times, even his eagerness) to take chances. He is the high-wire performer who draws in the crowd not simply because he balances sixty feet up without a net but because he keeps making his act more and more dangerous, doing headstands, handstands, and toestands or hanging by one finger. Obviously, the risk is great, "but it's that kind of chance-taking that may lead to something perfectly amazing" (*Night*, p. 280). Of course, it may lead just as easily to something absurd, as it occasionally does, but that is part of the fascination, for the viewer as well as the performer.

His emphasis on reality notwithstanding, Dickey has never been one to court the quotidian. The routine of domestic life and the ordinary day-to-day task of walking through the world have never much interested him. That is why a poem like "The Hospital Window" ironically calls attention to itself, because it adheres to the commonplace. A man who has just visited his dying father in the hospital pauses in the middle of the street outside to wave to him and, with the traffic roaring all around him, waits for his wave to be returned. When his father waves back, the son takes it as a form of nonverbal communication, as a sign that the father is not afraid to die. Beginning and ending with the flat, unemotional statement, "I have just come down from my father," this poem draws as near to the straightforward, confessional style as Dickey gets.

Much more representative of Dickey's poetry overall is "The Sheep Child," which stands as a model for other Dickey poems. Its sensational topic, which provoked objection from some audiences in the 1960s, still has the power to unsettle the even more tolerant and "worldly" readers of the 1980s. Focusing on the offspring of a sexual encounter between a human and a sheep, the poem definitely has "presentational immediacy," if not simple shock value. The sheep child speaks most of the poem from inside its jar of alcohol in an Atlanta museum, a narrative strategy that has led Dickey himself to say, half-jokingly, that he thinks the poem "can hardly be faulted from the standpoint of originality of viewpoint" (*SI*, p. 165).

But there is another speaker in the poem, a farm boy who has grown up believing in the myth of the sheep child and who lures the reader into the poem the way a good carnival barker pulls a crowd into the side show tent:

> I have heard tell
>
> That in a museum in Atlanta
> Way back in a corner somewhere
> There's this thing that's only half
> Sheep   like a woolly baby
> Pickled in alcohol   because
> Those things can't live   his eyes
> Are open   but you can't stand to look
> I heard from somebody who . . .
>
>   (*Poems*, p. 252)

By this point, readers are anxious to see this strange creature, and curiosity acts as the force to pull them along into the poem just as it would carry them past the gate and the tarpaulin flap at the county fair. The voice drawing them in is that of the pitchman, confident and confidential, saying what the farm boys say to "keep themselves off / Animals by legends of their own" (*Poems*, p. 252). The tone is that of the insider, of the one who has been there and knows and cannot disbelieve the legend, wondering,

> Are we,
> Because we remember, remembered
> In the terrible dust of museums?
> (*Poems*, p. 252)

An irresistible momentum is created by the absence of end punctuation and by the heavy enjambment in the first two stanzas, effects that contribute greatly to the reader's involvement in the poem. An air of complicity, of being party to an astonishing revelation, makes each of us as attentive as a farm boy hearing the tale for the first time "In the hay-tunnel dark / And dung of barns." The entire poem leading up to the sheep child's monologue has a sotto voce quality, underscored by the repetition immediately before the creature speaks:

> Merely with his eyes, the sheep-child may
> Be saying   saying
> (*Poems*, p. 252)

This is vintage Dickey style, using repetition as a suspense builder, as an eerie fanfare to introduce the sheep child we've all been waiting to encounter. If the voice here sounds like the one used by children when telling ghost stories, the resemblance is no accident. In fact, the entire poem follows the ghost story pattern, complete with the unidentified source of information whose accuracy and veracity are implicitly beyond question: "I heard from somebody who . . . ." And when the sheep child finally talks, he speaks in the other-worldly voice appropriate to telepathic communication from within a bottle of formaldehyde. The sheep child's speech is set in italics, presumably to emphasize its eeriness even further.

What Dickey employs in "The Sheep Child" and in many

other poems is a kind of folk narrative, story-telling characterized by its simplicity and straightforwardness. Because of its casual directness, "The Sheep Child" disarms and engages the reader with the immediacy of an oral presentation. Anyone within earshot would probably draw near to hear such a tale, just as most who start reading the poem find themselves swept along from line to line. Dickey intends to do more than startle; he uses the opportunity, after he has gained our attention, to explore one of his favorite themes—the relationship between the animal and human worlds. The sheep child is significant not as a grotesque mutation but as a privileged creature who "*saw for a blazing moment / The great grassy world from both sides*" (*Poems*, p. 253). Having a complete understanding of both "*Man and beast in the round of their need*," the creature possesses the kind of unified vision Dickey seeks throughout his work.

Except in those poems in which Dickey is self-hypnotized by the magical potential of the lyric, he avoids having what he once claimed to hate: a first line that "announces itself as 'poetry'" and "a special kind of poetry-language" (*Sorties*, p. 45). In his strongest narrative poems, Dickey deliberately works against the blatantly poetic to make his poems accessible to the broadest possible audience. How he sets out to do this is described in the following journal excerpt from *Sorties*:

> What we need, as *our* breakthrough, is a poetry of extreme simplicity, where one thing is said per line; but that thing must almost have infinite reverberations. I am not talking about a gnomic sort of utterance, but some new, modern thing. The sources of language for this sort of poetry have hardly been tapped at all. But if we can get this, poetry will have a great deal more resonance for people who never read much poetry because of the excesses of Berryman or the erudition of Empson. We need to go a different way from that now. I suspect that narrative may also have something to do with it, and if one could combine this extreme simplicity of utterance with a great deal of penetration and a narrative

element of either an ultra-real or a surreal kind, he would have what is going to be the wave of the future. Either he would have it, or he would make it. (*Sorties*, p. 106)

These observations prescribe exactly the kind of poetry found in "The Sheep Child." In his reference to Berryman and Empson, Dickey implicitly sets up these two poets as representatives of the extreme camps of confessionalism and formalism. His objective, however, is not to locate himself somewhere on the plain between but to find entirely new ground. As in "The Sheep Child," he wants poetry that is neither allusive nor confessional and that has a strong narrative component focusing on the "ultra-real" or surreal. Of significance, too, is his emphasis on accessibility and audience appeal. He wants poetry that sells itself to the reader.

Dickey's fascination with the surreal or the "ultra-real" introduces into his work the Southern Gothic element found in the fiction of writers like Eudora Welty and Flannery O'Connor. In his story of the sheep child, Dickey uses Southern mythology much the same way Welty uses it in "The Wide Net," in which a Loch Ness-like monster, rising from the river being seined for someone presumed drowned, is proclaimed King of the Snakes. Dickey's creature is as fantastic as Welty's and challenges credibility in much the same way. Curiously, both Dickey's half-sheep, half-human animal and Welty's enormous serpent remain remotely believable; we want to believe in them or cannot believe strongly enough in their impossibility. Because of their mythic proportions, they stand outside life.

The Gothic, among other elements, makes Dickey a much more Southern writer than anyone, including Dickey himself, has acknowledged. Though he has said, "It's important to me to be a Southerner" (*SI*, p. 35), he has qualified that assertion by insisting, "I would not under any circumstances want to feel that I was limited in any way by being a Southerner, that I was expected, say, by other people to indulge in the kind of regional chauvinism that has sometimes been indulged in by Southern writers" (*Night*, p. 253).

Such loud objections to the regional label have obscured Dickey's true and important kinship to the best writers of the South, particularly the fiction writers. Far from indulging in "regional chauvinism," Dickey has adopted a narrative view that aligns him with those Southern writers who transcend their region by using it rather than ignoring it. Consequently, if the sheep child, looking out from its jar in the museum, reminds us of Enoch Emery's "new Jesus" in *Wise Blood*, an embalmed pygmy who also resides behind glass in a museum, the similarities reveal a shared perception of the bizarre and its mythic potential within the context of the South.

Another poem that calls to mind *Wise Blood* is "A Folk Singer of the Thirties," whose speaker, like O'Connor's Hazel Motes, finds himself preaching something he finally cannot believe. For Motes it is the Church Without Christ, but for Dickey's unnamed speaker it is the philosophy of capitalistic expansion. In both instances, the character attains vision after undergoing a physical ordeal. In Motes's case, true vision is received in the end only after he blinds and disfigures himself with lye; while Dickey's folksinger has a clear perception of America (a perception he later corrupts) through the spikes driven into his hands and feet as he rocks across the country after being nailed to the outside of a boxcar by railroad guards. The Gothic element, present in much of Dickey's poetry, functions just as it does in the works of fiction writers who have been labeled Southern.

Dickey finds in his folksinger a character who is also an adept pitchman. In fact, he resembles an evangelical preacher, especially in the following passage:

> One night, I addressed the A.A.,
> Almost singing,
> And in the fiery,
> Unconsummated desire
> For drink that arose around me
> From those mild-mannered men,
> I mentioned a place for a shoe store

That I had seen near the yards
As a blackened hulk with potential.

A man rose up,
Took a drink from a secret bottle,
And hurried out of the room.
A year later to the day
He knelt at my feet
In a silver suit of raw silk.

(Poems, p. 152)

Recalling a talk delivered in a Hooverville, in "a chapel of galvanized tin," the speaker is once again caught up in the evangelical mood. His personal anecdote reflects a stock device used by revivalists, the confidential telling of some story of success or misery to get the crowd emotionally charged. In this case, the folksinger's sermon is not about religious faith but about financial success, a special kind of American salvation as remote as heaven during the depressed thirties.

The A.A. sermon is only one part of a larger personal anecdote, the story of the speaker's enlightenment and subsequent disillusionment. The entire poem is a kind of sermon, although spoken from the folksinger's apartment. Waking "not buried in pebbles / Behind the tank car, / But in the glimmering steeple," the speaker finds himself transformed from the boxcar rider in touch with the power and potential of America to a kind of media preacher who has sold his vision for profit. The poem, then, is his confession that something has gone wrong.

Though "A Folk Singer of the Thirties" is weak in some respects, particularly in the way its ending pulls up short, its great strength lies in its narrative style. In the folksinger turned preacher, Dickey discovered a voice with considerable power, one that blends the lyrical talent of the singer with the preacher's gift for extemporaneous speaking. The result is a short-line poem with the compelling power of a song created as it is sung or a sermon delivered spontaneously.

As Thomas O. Sloan has noted, "Dickey has a deep

sense of what speech, the spoken word, is."[3] I would go further and say that Dickey, in all but his most recent poems, has been preoccupied with getting the spoken word onto the page without doing it too much damage. Of course, whenever speech is transformed into print it changes, but Dickey's special mission as a poet has been to discover ways to minimize those alterations. Whether in the casual, conversational style of poems like "The Performance" or in the more insistent diction of "A Folk Singer of the Thirties," his objective has been to escape the restrictions of "poetic" language, or to expand the boundaries of what may be considered poetic. This is the direction he sought, away from Berryman and Empson toward a "simplicity of utterance," and his search led him not only to the sermon-ballad but to other forms as well, including the pure sermon, third-person narratives, and dramatic structures that resemble transcriptions of dialogue.

The pure sermon is represented by "May Day Sermon to the Women of Gilmer County, Georgia, by a Woman Preacher Leaving the Baptist Church." Modestly understating the poem's dimensions, Dickey has called "May Day Sermon" "just a retelling of a local folk myth" (*SI*, p. 184). The story that forms the text for the woman preacher's sermon is simple: a young woman kills her father and elopes with her lover after the father has cruelly beaten her for suspected sexual encounters with the young man. But such a brief plot summary fails to do justice either to the Gothic nature of the story itself or to the way the story is told; and the telling, in this poem, is everything. According to Dickey, what he hoped to capture in the narrative was language "which has a kind of unbridled frenzy about it, something like that frenzy found when a preacher—particularly of the rural, Baptist variety—works himself up into a state of fanatical, Biblical, unbridled frenzy" (*SI*, p. 184).

Swept up in the spirit and emotion of telling the women of Gilmer County "to throw off the shackles of the Baptist

3. Thomas O. Sloan, "The Open Poem is a Now Poem: Dickey's May Day Sermon," in *James Dickey: The Expansive Imagination*, ed. Richard J. Calhoun (Deland, Fla.: Everett/Edwards, 1973), pp. 85–86.

religion and enter into an older world of springtime, pleasure, love and delight" (*SI*, p. 184), the woman preacher attains the extreme height of religious fervor, as revealed in the following passage:

Listen   listen like females
     each year
In May   O glory   to the sound   the sound of your
     man gone wild
With love in the woods   let your nipples rise   and
     leave your feet
To hear: This is when moths flutter in from the open,
     and Hell
Fire of the oil lamp shrivels them   and it is said
To her: said like the Lord's voice trying to find a way
Outside the Bible   O sisters   O women and children
     who will be
Women of Gilmer County   you farm girls and Ellijay
     cotton mill
Girls, get up   each May Day   up in your socks   it
     is the father
Sound   going on about God   making, a hundred feet
     down,
The well beat its bucket like a gong.

(*Poems*, pp. 8-9)

The cadences of impassioned speech, with its repetitions—"Listen listen . . . to the sound   the sound"—and exhortations—"O sisters   O women"—place the readers in the congregation and invite them to be carried along on the pure flow of spontaneous language.

Though not alone in criticizing this poem, Paul Ramsey has made some of the most caustic remarks about it. Calling "May Day Sermon" a "very bad poem" resulting from "a failure in understanding the principles by which good or great long poems are possible," Ramsey invites a comparison of Dickey's poem and "The Eve of Saint Agnes," which he sees as similar to "May Day Sermon" in plot line but superior as poetry.[4] The problem with Ramsey's view is that it fails, or refuses, to allow Dickey the latitude he re-

4. Ramsey, "James Dickey: Meter and Structure," pp. 193–94.

quires. The Spenserian stanza used by Keats in his poem, whatever its qualities may be, is as far from what Dickey wants to do as grits are from tapioca. Consequently, if the poem fails according to the standards of the traditional long poem in English, that is because Dickey deliberately departs from tradition. The excesses and inconsistencies that trouble Ramsey and cause him to dislike "May Day Sermon" are natural elements of speech intensified by passion, not the flaws of a failed neoromantic narrative poem. Dickey is after reader involvement, not formalistic niceties.

On the page, the lines of "May Day Sermon" reach from margin to margin and are characterized by occasional gaps or spaces between words and phrases. The effect is not the same as that of prose, though the lines create a fairly dense block. In talking about this lining, Dickey has said, "I wanted to present the reader with solid and all but impenetrable walls—a wall of language in which you have these interstices of blank spaces at irregular places. It's a wall you can't get over, but you have to descend, climb down, in a way" (*Night*, p. 224). At the same time, the manner of presentation is intended to approximate the way the mind functions, sometimes hesitating, sometimes rushing forward. Overall, the poem has the appearance of a literal transcription of a sermon, with spaces inserted by the transcriber to denote pauses and associational shifts. Like most transcriptions of speech, this one is easier to follow if read aloud to reproduce, as much as possible, the quality of the original presentation. In fact, it seems reasonable to assert, as Thomas O. Sloan has done, that "the poem defies a silent perusal of its words on the printed page. It demands an oral reading."[5] If this is so, then Dickey has attained the kind of "presentational immediacy" he desires in his work. By making the reader a participant in the poem to the extent of obligating him to read it aloud, Dickey has found the perfect way to retain the dynamic qualities of speech within the context of a printed poem.

"Falling," another long poem that has provoked a di-

5. Sloan, "The Open Poem is a Now Poem," p. 88.

vided critical response, resembles "May Day Sermon": the page is dominated by the same long, split lines, and the language has the quality of extemporaneous speech. But here the narration is third person and the speaker has no clear identity. Consequently, the voice is disembodied and, probably, more poetic than Dickey would have wished. Though the story of the airline stewardess is certainly dramatic, the poem lacks a dramatic context, like the sermon, within which the story can be presented. Thus, there is no obvious dynamic situation into which the reader can enter as complete participant. Even so, this poem also insists on an oral reading, especially because it is so fluid. With only ten end punctuation marks in the entire narrative, the story rushes or plummets toward its conclusion, just as the stewardess falls precipitously to her death. Yet this momentum can only be guessed at through a silent reading; it must be sensed through oral participation in order to be experienced and appreciated fully.

In "May Day Sermon," the myth of the young woman who murders her father and rides off on the risen ghostly roads of creeks with her lover is subordinate to the sermon within which it is presented. Its function is to help the woman preacher get across her message to the women of Gilmer County. In "Falling," however, the myth of the stewardess turned goddess in free-fall over Kansas is primary. Although the narrator stands between us and the stewardess's experience, he does not comment to any great extent on what her fall and her actions before impact might imply. We are left to find our own applications for the myth, and the process involves us even more deeply in the poem. Looked at side by side, these two poems represent variations on a single narrative experiment, as Dickey tests his open, speechlike forms in first- and third-person voices.

The same kind of experimentation is sustained in "The Fiend" and "The Eye-Beaters," each focusing on the psychology of a particular type of societal misfit. "The Fiend" employs a third-person narrative to describe the obsessed behavior of a homicidal Peeping Tom who watches from trees and bushes as women dress, undress, and go about their private lives. In form and point of view, this poem greatly resembles "Falling," and the split-line style is particularly well-suited to the psychotic personality under scrutiny. Similar in style, "The Eye-Beaters" is a curious mixture of third and first person, along with marginal summaries of the type found in some nineteenth-century novels. Under examination here are blind children who beat their eyes in order to "see" something—light, perhaps—but the speaker, imagining much more, fantasizes that they are able to attain a vision of prehistory, when the human race was young. Swinging back and forth between reason and invention, the speaker engages in a kind of internal dialogue, sometimes assessing things from the objective, reasoned distance of third-person, and sometimes being swept up in the subjectivity of first-person involvement.

Dickey seeks in all his split-line, open-form poems (with the exception of "The Shark's Parlor," which is a straightforward first-person tale) an approximation of how the mind works. In "May Day Sermon," the mind is literally spoken, but in "Falling," "The Fiend," and "The Eye-Beaters" the story is internalized as an omniscient narrator delves into the conscious and unconscious minds of people under stress: a dying woman, a voyeur, and a visitor to a home for blind children (who happens also to be the narrator). In "Falling" and "The Fiend," the narrator comes between the poem's central character and the reader, eliminating the possibility of speech. But as the mixture of third and first person in "The Eye-Beaters" illustrates, Dickey is interested not only in speech projected outward but also in the kind of internal conversations we all experience, those running dialogues in which we ask ourselves, as if we were someone else, "Why did you do that?" or "What will you do now?" This is precisely the disembodied voice that inhabits "Falling" and whose detached but involved observations are ended by the first-person exclamation of the stewardess ("Ah God—") as she dies. It is the objective center in each of us that watches and, if called upon, could voice our secrets in its strangely distant yet intimate way, just as the voyeur's secrets are disclosed in "The Fiend."

All of this shows how fascinated Dickey has been with narrative technique as a device to involve the reader and thereby sell the poem. The fictional element in such narrative experimentation is strong, and so Dickey's poems often resemble stories. This is particularly true in poems that employ dialogue, "Mercy," for example:

> The girls that went up are coming
> Down, turning the leaves
> Of the sign-out book. You waiting for Fay? Yes.
> She'll be a little while. O.K.
> More ice, to ice-pack
> The gin. The last door opens.
> It is Fay.[6]

Except for the odd spacing, Dickey's deliberate movement away from the split-line toward a poem balanced on the page, this could be prose, and so could the following passage from "Looking for the Buckhead Boys":

> Mr. Hamby, remember me?
>   God A'Mighty! Ain't you the
> one
> Who fumbled the punt and lost the Russell game?
>   That's right.
>   How're them butter fingers?
>   Still butter, I say,
> Still fumbling. But what about the rest of the team?
>   (*Motion*, p. 18)

In these poems, Dickey has moved so far away from the lyrical that one feels compelled to ask if they are poems at all. The narrative element is everything, and some of the dialogue thumps as flat as bad prose. The danger in trying to reclaim some of the territory lost by poetry to the novel and short story is that one may take back too much and

6. James Dickey, *The Central Motion: Poems, 1968–1979* (Middletown, Conn.: Wesleyan University Press, 1983), p. 11. Cited hereafter as *Motion* in text.

end up writing prose, which happens to Dickey on occasion.

At the outer extreme of Dickey's narrative experimentation and his dangerous attraction to the prosier aspects
of fiction lies *The Zodiac*, the book-length rantings of a
drunken Dutch poet, loosely framed within the comments
of a third-person narrator. For fifty-three pages, the Dutch-
man hallucinates and rambles his way toward an understanding of the universe and his place in it. Dickey's admission that much of *The Zodiac* "is maundering, a lot of it is
foolish and self-delusionary" (*Night*, p. 223) can be cor-
roborated by almost any random passage:

> You talk about *looking*: Would you look at *that*
> Electric page! What the hell did I say? Did *I* say that?
> You bastard, you. Why didn't you know that before?
> Where the hell have you been with your *head*?
> You and the paper should have known it, you and the ink:
> you write
>
> Everybody writes
>
> With blackness. Night. Why has it taken you all this time?
> All this travel, all those lives
> You've fucked up?
>
> (*Motion*, p. 70)

Though other parts of *The Zodiac* manifest a bit more sensitivity to the sounds and nuances of words, there is absolutely nothing lyrical about this passage. The uninteresting
language is matched by the banality of the idea it carries.
The notion that black words on white paper are mystically
symbolic is the kind of overblown connection that only
a drunk (or perhaps a Byronic thirteen-year-old) would
make.

Dickey claims to like *The Zodiac* because "it is such an un-
well-made piece of work." Further, he says, "I think that if
I haven't done anything else in *The Zodiac* I have truly
keyed-in on one of the most important things in the relationship of a person to his own poetry—and that is the
combination of foolishness, daring and self-delusion that is
necessary to make memorable poetry" (*Night*, p. 223). His

emphasis is not so much on the poem itself as on the attitude that made the poem possible in the first place; and he is saying that memorable poetry may yet be written, if *The Zodiac* should not succeed, simply because he possesses the necessary drive and bravado. In short, he is willing to take chances, to strike out in new and different directions "even if it's a long and costly mistake" (*Night*, p. 321). But while Dickey's courage may be admirable, some of its products are not. Still, the consummate pitchman has often obscured the distinction between nobility of effort and quality of product, so much so that a terribly flawed, adolescent poem like *The Zodiac* has been admired by some critics not because of the poet's accomplishment but because of his intent.

Most of Dickey's experimentation is aesthetically pure; it apparently proceeds from a genuine desire to break through to new, unexplored territory. But some of his efforts took a decidedly commercial turn in the 1970s as Dickey began literally selling his work, marketing poems as if he were working once more for the advertising firm of Burke Dowling Adams, which he left in 1961. Two such packaged poems appear in the 1970 volume *The Eye-Beaters, Blood, Victory, Madness, Buckhead, and Mercy* but were first published in a popular magazine, *Life*. One of them, "Apollo" was written to commemorate the moon landing and is better than MacLeish's poem ("Voyage to the Moon") on the subject, though not so good as Auden's cynical view in "Moon Landing." Another, "In the Pocket," originally published as part of a National Football League section of *Life*, illustrates all that is bad about occasional poetry as Dickey has his quarterback speak these lines:

> Around me the wrong color
> Is looming   hands are coming
> Up and over between
> My Arm and Number Three: throw it hit him in the middle
> Of his enemies   hit move scramble
> Before death and the ground

> Come up   LEAP STAND KILL DIE STRIKE
> Now.
>
> *(Motion*, p. 32)

Such hyperbolic screaming must strike even the professional quarterbacks of the NFL as ridiculous. After all, football is only a game and, Dickey's assertions notwithstanding, not even a very apt metaphor for life. Moreover, one wonders how it is possible to leap then stand, kill then die, and still be able to strike.

Four other occasional poems appear in *The Strength of Fields* (1979), among them the title poem, which was read at Jimmy Carter's presidential inaugural celebration and, with its emphasis on kindness as the saving grace of humanity, stresses the simple virtues of humankind. Almost as effective is "Exchanges," delivered as the 1970 Phi Beta Kappa poem for Harvard University and not terribly dated despite its topical references to environmental pollution and the Apollo moon missions. Embarrassingly maudlin, however, is an elegy "For the Death of Lombardi"—not quite as bad as "In the Pocket" but almost—with its imagery of middle-aged beer guzzlers looking to Vince Lombardi as to Christ, who must surely rise and win. And trite beyond explanation is "For the Running of the New York City Marathon," which celebrates the event by dubbing every finisher a winner, a tedious tribute that must have been spoken at some point by every television sportscaster who has been given time on the air.

These half-dozen poems are worth noting not because of their quality, as should be obvious, but because they reveal the extent of Dickey's drive to sell the poem. It is possible that the level of Dickey's writing in a poem like "In the Pocket" was deliberately kept within reach of the broadest possible audience because Dickey wanted every television viewing football fan who might pick up a copy of the poem in *Life* to be able to comprehend it. But such mass marketing is bound to produce inferior poetry, regardless of its public relations value on the grand scale; the serious poet cannot long pursue the lowest-common-denominator style without selling his artistic soul in the bargain. At his best, Dickey has sold the poem through his serious pursuit of the narrative and his search for ways to involve the reader in the poetry. At his worst, he has lowered his standards of quality and sold a cheaper product.

IV. Selling God

During his years in the corporate offices of advertising, Dickey's unflagging loyalty to poetry made him a double agent, as he spirited books into the corridors of product promotion and secretly worked on drafts of poems on company time. Once, he was reprimanded by a superior for reading poetry instead of sales reports during lunch (*Night*, p. 352), but the most telling encounter between artist and ad agency is captured in the following Dickey anecdote:

> I wrote this poem ["The Heaven of Animals"] in an advertising office. I had a new secretary and I asked her to type it for me. She typed up the poem letter-perfect and brought it to me. Then she asked, "What is it? What company does it go to?"
> "This is a poem," I said.
> "It is?"
> "Yes, it is, I hope."
> "What are we going to sell with it?" she asked.
> "God," I said. "We're going to sell God."
>
> (*SI*, p. 108)

This humorous story, with its satirical jabs at the secretary's lamentable, one-dimensional view of things, has a serious thrust as well. The joke may be on the secretary, but Dickey's assertion is more than mock-serious; it is self-revelatory, for behind the rhetorical packaging and the verbal manipulations, a Dickey poem is usually intended to sell God.

Dickey's pitch for God is made in the voice of the visionary, or would-be visionary, who is engaged in a kind of mystical quest for wholeness. His search may lead him toward lower animal or higher spiritual forms, but the objective is always the same—to attain an elevation of awareness and a perception of the coherent universe. Viewed in broad terms, the quest is religious in nature, though it is not tied to any particular religion. Rather, it reflects Dickey's own unique religion, a combination of the primitive, animistic, and highly personal elements, which he has summed up in this way:

> What I want more than anything else is to have a feeling of wholeness. Specialization has produced some extremely important things, like penicillin and heart transplants. But I don't know how much they compensate for the loss of a sense of intimacy with the natural process. I think you would be very hard-put, for example, to find a more harmonious relationship to an environment than the American Indians had. We can't return to a primitive society; surely this is obvious. But there is a property of the mind which, if encouraged, could have this personally animistic relationship to things. (*SI*, p. 68)

Dickey explores within himself and nurtures in his readers that "property of the mind" that can bridge the divisions between self and other, that can bring about a harmonious relationship with the natural world.

Unlike Theodore Roethke, the poet Dickey claims to admire the most, whose mystical quest took the symbolic forms of an arduous journey away from the physical limitations of the body and of a perilous internal exploration of the sub- and preconscious mind, Dickey comes by his revelations without effort. And while Roethke's push was always toward the Absolute, the One that subsumes everything and in which all individual identities are abandoned, Dickey's quest falls far short of any such terrifying union. For those who imagine that illumination and a sense of wholeness are won at the price of spiritual and emotional exertion, Dickey's attainment of vision comes all too easily. Howard Nemerov recognized this in a 1963 review of *Drowning With Others* when he identified "the language of a willed mysticism" in some of Dickey's poems.[1] Though Roethke can make us believe he has seen the blinding illumination, the brilliant darkness of the Ultimate One, it is

1. Howard Nemerov, "Poems of Darkness and a Specialized Light," in *The Imagination as Glory: The Poetry of James Dickey*, ed. Bruce Weigl and T. R. Hummer (Urbana: University of Illinois Press, 1984), p. 13.

difficult to believe Dickey has had a similar experience. In fact, it seems likely that Dickey has gone no further than the faint stirrings we all feel from time to time, the sensation of a reality beyond what we normally perceive as real. Even so, he has tried to will himself beyond the phenomenal world.

Dickey's greatest gift as a poet is his ability to commit himself entirely to his invention. By "*giving* himself to his invention which, with luck, is also his vision" (*SI*, p. 91), the poet may succeed in making his fiction true. Not coincidentally, this is also one of the pitchman's most important talents, the ability to sell himself on his product before he tries to sell it to anyone else. In this way, Dickey has literally made his own truth and willed himself farther down the road of mystical vision than he has actually been able to travel. Because Dickey seems so genuinely to believe in his accounts of wholeness, it is difficult for the reader to dismiss them as false or shallow, even when they seem more comic than cosmic. When the man in the plaid suit stands beside a car that probably wouldn't make it off the lot under its own power and says, with utter conviction, "It runs a lot better than it looks. I drove it home and back to work at lunch today," something in most of us wants to believe him.

"Springer Mountain" is an excellent example of Dickey's willed mysticism. Focusing on a forty-year-old hunter, alone at dawn with his bow and arrows (à la Dickey himself), stalking the big-racked buck, the poem uses the old cliche of the hunter so overcome by the beauty of his prey that he cannot fire. But in this case, Dickey gives the old line a new knot: the middle-aged hunter inexplicably begins pulling off his clothes and running through the woods after the deer he has been unable to shoot. In defense of this poem, which has been the object of considerable derision, Dickey rationalizes thus: "As Longinus points out, there's a razor's edge between sublimity and absurdity. And that's the edge I try to walk. Sometimes *both* sides are ludicrous! You have to risk people saying, 'That's the silliest goddamn thing I ever read!' But I don't think you can get to sublimity without courting the ridiculous" (*SI*, p. 65).

He slants the argument, of course. Another view might hold that the way to the sublime is true, while the road to the false sublime has numerous way stations marked *ridiculous*. Still, Dickey believes himself to be on the right highway; he wills it so, and the force of his conviction carries weight, even when his poems fall short of their sublime objective. In "Springer Mountain," the sense of communion between man and deer seems entirely manufactured by the poet, and the poem itself fails to offer sufficient motivation for the symbolic act of disrobing in an effort to return to the natural world; yet many readers still credit Dickey for his brave push toward sublimity.

Dickey's weak defense of this weak poem has the petulant tone of an artist who feels mistreated by cynical critics. Saying, as Dickey does, that anything can appear silly depending on how it is perceived is the kind of relative equivocation that calls to mind its counterpoint: anything can appear serious, depending on how it is perceived. The burden, then, is on the perceiver, and Dickey places it solidly there by saying, "So much depends not only upon how you look at things, but how capable you are of participating in them" (*SI*, p. 66). Dickey expects his readers to give themselves to the poem with an abandon equal to his own commitment, but the fulfillment of that expectation hinges on the poem's "presentational immediacy." No matter how inclined readers may be to suspend disbelief, they depend heavily on the poet's assistance, on the persuasiveness of his pitch. Consequently, when a poem like "Springer Mountain" fails, the ultimate responsibility for that failure lies with the poet, not the reader.

Though "Springer Mountain" is crippled by Dickey's poor execution of his material, the ultimate flaw lies in the material itself. A statement from *Sorties*, presented with the directness of absolute truth, helps to explain this situation: "The first prerequisite for a great poem is a great *concept* for a poem" (*Sorties*, p. 96). However, many great poems have derived from other sources, from language it-self, for example, from an image or a phrase that accretes more language until a concept is evolved. Yet it seems that most of Dickey's poems have originated as ideas for poems. While there is nothing wrong with this approach, it makes considerable demands on the poet's ability to surrender to the idea, to discover the necessary spontaneity of insight to make the poem live. When the poet fails to find what Dickey has identified as the proper "combination of will, intelligence, and abandon" (*Sorties,* p. 72), he is left with mostly will, mostly intelligence, or mostly abandon, and the poem presents itself primarily as an unrealized idea. So it is with "Springer Mountain."

As H. L. Weatherby has pointed out in his valuable essay "The Way of Exchange in James Dickey's Poetry," Dickey's straining after the mystical has left him vulnerable to the criticism he himself leveled at his contemporaries in *The Suspect in Poetry,* that most of them contrive too much and fail to make their poems believable.[2] Dickey is brought to this point of indirect self-criticism by the mistaken notion that a mystical perception of the world can be willed. Al-though a person may make himself ready for and receptive to mystical vision, the apprehension itself is nonvolitional. The most remarkable quality of Dickey's perceptions of wholeness is that they attain any level of credibility at all. Should his moments of illumination remain mere philo-sophical formulations, it would be less surprising. But Dickey is able to abandon himself to his idea, once he has willed it, compensating for a lack of spontaneity with the energy of his commitment. There is bound to be something stimulating about a poet determined to "follow my im-pulses to some kind of *reductio ad absurdum*" (*SI,* p. 155). The exhilaration of the roller coaster ride takes precedence over the badly painted Alpine scenery that forms a back-ground for the tracks.

"Approaching Prayer" is also a poem that stretches cred-

2. H. L. Weatherby, "The Way of Exchange in James Dickey's Poetry," in *James Dickey: The Expansive Imagination*, ed. Richard J. Calhoun (Deland, Fla.: Everett/Edwards, 1973), p. 64.

ibility thinner than blown glass. When the speaker costumes himself in his father's old sweater, gamecock spurs, and a boar's head, he appears ridiculous and laughable rather than transcendent. Ironically, though, the poem works precisely because of the speaker's preposterous actions, works not as a moment of mystical illumination but as an example of how one may go about willing such a vision, or something resembling it. He begins in this way:

> And I must get up and start
> To circle through my father's empty house
> Looking for things to put on
> Or to strip myself of
> So that I can fall to my knees
> And produce a word I can't say
> Until all my reason is slain.
>
> (*Poems*, p. 163)

Realizing that true vision can come about only through subordination of the logical, analytical mind and elevation of the intuitive faculties, the son engages in a process of ritual magic. Circling in his father's house and symbolically changing identity by putting something on or stripping it off are initial steps in the effort to slay reason.

After he collects the items he thinks he will need—boar's head, spurs, and sweater—he places them on a chair in the attic of the empty house and, feeling nothing, concludes, "Perhaps I should feel more foolish, / Even, than this" (*Poems*, p. 163). The speaker's curious equation of feeling foolish with attaining some kind of illumination affords a key to Dickey's attraction to the bizarre and the ridiculous. Like the poem's speaker, Dickey believes that the rational mind can be overcome with absurdity, that the absurd truly is the way to the sublime. For the young man in the poem, donning his preposterous outfit does indeed bring him a vision. Standing in the attic, dressed like some primitive tribesman who knows less of the brain than of the blood, he sees what the boar saw when he killed it.

When the vision is over, the speaker takes off his magical costume and leaves the house, reflecting:

> I don't know quite what has happened
> Or that anything has,
>
> Hoping only that
> The irrelevancies one thinks of
> When trying to pray
> Are the prayer,
>
> And that I have got by my own
> Means to the hovering place
>   (*Poems*, p. 167)

The "desert fathers" invoked at the end of the poem are the genuine visionaries who saw angels and prophesied. Not privileged to be among the true seers, the speaker hopes to have found his own way to illumination and understanding.

Read as an adumbration of Dickey's strategy to push through to a vision of wholeness and coherence, to rise to the "hovering place," "Approaching Prayer" helps to clarify many things, particularly his fondness for the absurd. Subduing the rational mind through absurd, nonrational behavior is not as subtle as the technique of meditation, but it is not so far removed from the strategy of the koan. Eastern contemplatives have long known that the analytical part of the mind can be quieted by focusing it on a koan, a question or puzzle that has no logical answer or explanation. By dwelling on a fundamentally absurd question—such as "What is the sound of the color blue?"—one can slay reason. Dickey's angle, as in "Approaching Prayer," is more directly absurd, but his objective is the same as for users of the koan: to subdue reason and heighten intuition and imagination.

What all of this means is that Dickey has no desire to make his bizarre, exotic details realistic or believable on a rational plane. Instead, he means for them to remain outrageous, even ludicrous. After all, Dickey seeks full reader participation, and if readers are to experience whatever perception the poem offers, they must also subdue the rational mind. Such an approach demands a great deal from the reader, a more complete giving over than most are willing or able to accomplish.

However, Dickey the shaman does not always appear clad in boar's head, tattered sweater, and cock spurs. In "Encounter in the Cage Country" he wears ordinary clothing and a pair of green sunglasses; still, his objective, as in "Approaching Prayer," is to conjure some glimpse of wholeness. Like the boar's head, the sunglasses gain him admission into the world of animals and put him in touch, momentarily, with the "forfeited animal grace of human beings" (*Babel*, p. 291). Thus, the voice at the end of the poem, which seems to be the collective spirit of the natural world, says:

> *Your moves are exactly right*
> *For a few things in this world: we know you*
> *When you come, Green Eyes, Green Eyes.*
> (*Poems*, p. 275)

As in "Approaching Prayer," the speaker does something foolish to trick his rational mind. Here, before the panther's cage, he puts on a kind of slapstick routine, "first saunt'ring then stalking / Back and forth like a sentry" (*Poems*, p. 274). To the great amusement of the children looking on, he even fakes a run and pretends to draw a gun from an imaginary holster on his hip. Ironically, his actions make him the center of attention as he becomes the animal on view and symbolically changes places with the panther, who has become an attentive onlooker. His perception of the children as "bite-sized," just big enough to be a morsel for a panther, shows the extent of the interchange, for he sees the world as the caged animal sees it. When he walks away, the crowd quails from him as from a dangerous beast.

"Encounter In the Cage Country" is a more plausible poem than "Approaching Prayer" because the sense of communion with the animal world seems more the product of spontaneous insight than of willed vision or, in the case of "Springer Mountain," poetic manipulation. Of course, most of us may find the grown man's childish antics in front of the panther's cage a little bizarre; but even so, his behavior falls within the bounds of credibility. Like any good pitchman, Dickey knows just how far to push his claims before they will begin to seem outrageous and false. But unlike the typical salesman, he pushes up to the absolute limit, and sometimes beyond. When his poems work well, they do so because Dickey knows when to stop or finds a way to make the preposterous acceptable and the incredible believable. For example, most readers accept the half-sheep, half-human speaker in "The Sheep Child," contrary to all biological laws, because the creature's existence is validated only by hearsay and therefore is more mythic than real. This enables Dickey to conjure forth a sheep child and affords him an opportunity to present a hybrid view of the world, a view in which man and animal participate equally, made one in the short-lived "woolly baby." By maneuvering the reader into an acceptance of the sheep child, who is rationally unacceptable, Dickey makes possible some small participation in the creature's (and Dickey's own) perception of wholeness, which transcends the purely rational.

The difficulties facing the poet who strives toward a vision of wholeness with the intention of communicating what he sees and experiences are effectively considered in "A Dog Sleeping on My Feet." As the poet works late into the evening, carefully accommodating the dog on his feet, he realizes that what he has written in his notebook is not the poem he is after:

> The poem is beginning to move
> Up through my pine-prickling legs
> Out of the night wood,
>
> Taking hold of the pen by my fingers.
> (*Poems*, p. 55)

As his legs go numb, he participates in a dream the dog is having of pursuing a fox through the forest. The vision ends, however, "on the brightness of paper," when the poet's hand, "which speaks in a daze / The hypnotized language of beasts," falls "Back into the human tongue" (*Poems*, p. 55). The experience does not translate into human language because it is ineffable, beyond expression in mere words. Still, it is the poet's self-given duty to try to capture at least a vague sensation of his perception.

While this poem may seem a rationalization of failure, it is actually an explanation of Dickey's role as poet. As the "energized man," the poet is responsible not simply for seeking out meaning in life for himself but also for communicating some sense of the meaning he discovers. If the effort is foredoomed, it is nevertheless vitally important as a stand against the flatness and the incompleteness of human life. Dickey speaks as one come back from beyond the frontier bearing a message of wholeness and joy. The process is summarized by Dickey in a reference to Stanley Edgar Hyman's description of the rites of passage as "a separation from the world, a penetration to some source of power and a life enhancing return."[3] The coming back is at least as important as the getting there, for Dickey has a sense of mission. Consequently, although his poems may often challenge credibility, they seldom fail to carry a strong sense of conviction; the pitchman's belief in his own pitch helps sell it to others, even when it is cast in grandly preposterous dimensions.

The process Dickey wishes the reader to engage in is described straightforwardly in "Inside the River," which reads like a set of instructions:

> Step down.
> Follow your right
> Foot nakedly in
> To another body.
>   (*Poems*, p. 105).

By surrendering wholly to the river, one can create "A new, inner being," in touch with the whole world:

> Weight more changed
> Than that of one
> Now being born,
> Let go the root.
> Move with the world

3. Richard J. Calhoun and Robert W. Hill, *James Dickey* (Boston: G. K. Hall, 1983), p. 118.

As the deep dead move,
Opposed to nothing.
Release. Enter the sea
Like a winding wind.
No. Rise. Draw breath.
Sing. See no one.
                    (*Poems*, p. 106)

At the last moment, just before the individual identity is abandoned to the larger One, the spell must be broken and a return effected. To do otherwise is to choose death. The objective is to move to a source of power, here symbolized by the river, and then return to the world with a new vision.

The prescriptive tone of "Inside the River" is also found in "The Head-Aim," which tells how to become an animal and reveals "the whole secret of being / Inhuman" (*Poems*, p. 271). The trick is

                    to aim the head as you should,
And to hold back in the body
What the mouth might otherwise speak:
Immortal poems—those matters of life and death—
When the lips curl back

And the eyes prepare to sink
Also, in the jerking fur of the other.

Fox, marten, weasel,
No one can give you hands.
Let the eyes see death say it all
Straight into your oncoming face, the head
Not fail, not tell.

                    (*Poems*, p. 271)

To become inhuman is to become nonverbal, to express through the natural acts of the body in its life and death struggle the poems that might otherwise be spoken. The head, source of the intellect and of verbalization, must be aimed straight into the maw of death and give way entirely to the body.

If "Inside the River" and "The Head-Aim" tell the reader how to participate more fully in Dickey's pursuit of a vision of wholeness, they also tell Dickey himself just how far to go. In addition to their prescriptive qualities, both poems have a proscriptive element. In one case, Dickey tells himself directly not to yield to the impulse to become immersed entirely in the river. In the other, he implicitly warns himself off any desire to become inhuman by acknowledging that animals approach poetic expression only through their ongoing fight for survival. In order to speak or write poems, one must, after all, remain human. Like the hunter in "Springer Mountain," who understands that he must be "what I most am and should be / And can be only once in this life" (*Poems*, p. 132), and the writer in "A Dog Sleeping On My Feet," who comes home "From the dream of an animal, / Assembling the self I must wake to" (*Poems*, p. 56), Dickey accepts his role in life despite the strong impulse to lose himself in the natural world of animals.

Whatever mystical tendencies Dickey may have, he is finally a poet of illumination rather than union. He seeks a vision of wholeness, not a complete participation in the Great One that would involve giving up the self. He wants a personal view of the world enriched through imaginative perception, because "the imaginative conceiving and perceiving of a thing alters its reality for the observer: it is his way of possessing it, of installing it in a private Heaven."[4] Imagination, then, creates, in Dickey's terms, its own "Glory." Poetry, as a product of the imagination, can lead to a perception of wholeness that becomes an end in itself, its own kind of heaven; and that is why, finally, Dickey draws back from a surrender of self to the river or to the world of the animal. He believes he can move near enough to the brilliant heart of wholeness through his poetry to capture something of its essence. How successful he is depends entirely on how well he employs his imaginative powers.

Because the second person has been so incompetently used by so many contemporary poets, who introduce the

4. James Dickey, "The Imagination as Glory," in *The Imagination as Glory: The Poetry of James Dickey*, ed. Bruce Weigl and T. R. Hummer (Urbana: University of Illinois Press, 1984), p. 168.

pronoun *you* when they really mean *I* or when they don't know whom they mean, it is easy to mistake Dickey's use of it in "Inside the River" and "The Head-Aim" as slack or meaningless. But Dickey is not engaged in any false objectivity in these two poems; rather, he is directly addressing his readers and challenging them to become imaginatively involved in the pursuit of a sense of wholeness. Dickey knows that his own entry into the river and into the identity of fox, marten, or weasel would have less immediacy if the reader were to remain an objective outside observer.

Dickey uses the same device in "The Salt Marsh," placing the reader in the middle of a lake of sawgrass. Exactly head high, the tall stalks with their oversized blades prevent "you" from seeing over them or through them to find a way out of the marsh. As though chiding us to let go a little, Dickey says:

> And nothing prevents your bending
> With them, helping their wave
> Upon wave upon wave upon wave
> By not opposing,
> By willing your supple inclusion
> Among fields without promise of harvest,
> In their marvelous, spiritual walking
> Everywhere, anywhere.
>
> (*Poems,* p. 108)

This is a direct charge to the reader to overcome inhibitions and fears and, through the power of the imagination, to will participation in the sense of wholeness. After all, nothing prevents our "supple inclusion" but our own opposition.

Taken collectively, "Approaching Prayer," "A Dog Sleeping on My Feet," "Inside the River," "The Head-Aim," and "The Salt Marsh" reveal Dickey's strategy for selling God, or at least his individual notion of God. He subdues the rational mind through absurdity or through the workings of the imagination, enters into a perception of wholeness, and returns to tell what he has seen. Essential to the success of this process is reader involvement, which is at once the strong and weak point of the approach. If they can manage a reasonable level of participation in Dickey's perceptions, readers will find the poems effective and insightful; if they cannot involve themselves sufficiently, however, the poems will often remain absurd or silly. Dickey's strategy leaves no opportunity to stand back and assess things from a detached point of view. To comprehend as fully as possible we must will our "supple inclusion" in Dickey's "marvelous, spiritual walking."

Far from being orthodox, Dickey's view of God is pantheistic, as the following remarks illustrate:

> Religion to me involves myself and the universe, and it does not admit of any kind of intermediary, such as Jesus or the Bible. . . . But the religious sense, which seems to me very strong in my work in some weird kind of way, is a very personal kind of stick-and-stone religion. I would have made a great Bushman or an aborigine who believes that spirits inhabit all things. (*SI,* pp. 78-79)

To find God, one need not push through to some ethereal plane in pursuit of a graybeard or an abstraction but simply get in touch with the wholeness of the universe as it is manifested through the natural world. A weasel will do as well as a river, provided one has the necessary imaginative powers. In this respect, for Dickey, the imagination itself becomes a kind of religion, the way to the only certain glory, the world as we are able to perceive it or, in effect, create it.

"In the Mountain Tent" offers a complete embodiment of Dickey's search for wholeness. A man lies listening to the rain falling on his tent and believes it is "Laying down all around where I lie / A profound, unspeakable law" (*Poems,* p. 109). As with the person in the marsh grass, the proper thing to do is to yield to the dictates of nature, and so the speaker here obeys the law of the rain and finds himself

> free-falling slowly

> Through the thought-out leaves of the wood
> Into the minds of animals.
>
> (*Poems,* p. 109)

As in "The Head-Aim," the animal entered by the speaker in this poem

> thinks of a poem—
> Green, plausible, living, and holy—
> And cannot speak.
>
> (*Poems*, p. 109)

Lying still "as if recently killed," his brow "watermarked with the mark / On the wing of a moth," a sign of his passage into the natural world, the speaker feels "the tent taking shape on my body / Like ill-fitting, Heavenly clothes." Elevated by imagination to a vision of heaven, he is nonetheless unready to enter that realm himself, as the poorly fitting clothes reveal. Instead, he prepares for his return to the world of human perception:

> From holes in the ground comes my voice
> In the God-silenced tongue of the beasts.
> "I shall rise from the dead," I am saying.
>
> (*Poems*, p. 110)

Coming back, he brings with him a vision of wholeness, presumably the one described in the poem itself.

The dead figure prominently in Dickey's search for wholeness, simply because death has returned them to the elements from which they came and has made them once again integral to the universe. Though death itself holds some attraction, Dickey rejects it, relying instead on his imaginative ability to tap the spiritual beings of those already dead, and to return to the world with his vision. In this vein, three poems are of particular interest: "In the Tree House at Night," "Drinking from a Helmet," and "The Driver."

The prevailing spirit of "In the Tree House at Night" is that of Dickey's older brother Eugene, who died before Dickey was born. Lying in the tree, which lifts them literally above the earth, the speaker and his younger, sleeping brother sway amid leaves "That move with the moves of the spirit" (*Poems*, p. 66). Like some natural aeolian harp played upon by the breeze, the tree responds to the touch of the dead brother:

Wind springs, as my dead brother smiles
And touches the tree at the root;

A shudder of joy runs up
The trunk; the needles tingle;
One bird uncontrollably cries.
The wind changes round, and I stir
Within another's life. Whose life?
Who is dead? Whose presence is living?
                    (*Poems*, p. 67)

Huddled in his crude tree house, separated from the earth, the speaker becomes a part of the tree and feels the spiritual stirrings. So overwhelming is the sense of his dead brother's presence that the distinction between life and death becomes obscured and the speaker feels that he himself may be dead or that his brother may be living. By eliminating the barrier between life and death, Dickey attains another perception of wholeness, one familiar to students of mysticism.

The autobiographical material makes "In the Tree House at Night" seem more original than it is, drawing attention away from the poem's derivative nature, particularly in its final three stanzas, which conclude with the following series of questions:

Can two bodies make up a third?
To sing, must I feel the world's light?
My green, graceful bones fill the air
With sleeping birds
                    (*Poems*, p. 67)

These questions are strikingly similar to a series by Theodore Roethke in "Praise to the End":

Is the eternal near, fondling?
I hear the sound of hands.

Can the bones breathe? This grave has an ear.
It's still enough for the knock of a worm.[5]

5. Theodore Roethke, *The Collected Poems* (Garden City, N.Y.: Anchor/Doubleday, 1975), p. 83.

But the parallels are even more obvious between Dickey's ending:

> Alone, alone
> And with them I move gently.
> I move at the heart of the world
>
> (*Poems*, p. 67)

and Roethke's final lines for "A Field of Light": "And I walked, I walked through the light air; / I moved with the morning."[6]

Such stylistic and verbal similarities strongly suggest that Dickey may also have borrowed his vision from Roethke. In his effort to come to terms with the death of his brother, Dickey seems to have used Roethke's struggle to accept the death of a father in "The Lost Son" sequence as a model. Such emulation, especially when it approaches imitation, undermines the reader's ability to believe in the poem. For Dickey, who depends so heavily on reader involvement, this erosion of credibility equals the worst kind of failure.

Perhaps Dickey borrows so heavily from Roethke because he lacks the power himself to invoke the spirit of the dead and to merge with it. To be sure, when Dickey is entirely on his own in a poem like "Drinking from a Helmet," the evocation of a sense of union with the dead seems contrived and false. Even Dickey's bland paraphrase of the poem suggests something of its inadequacies: the soldier "dedicates himself to survival and to looking up the brother of the dead soldier whose last thought he inherited by drinking from the dead man's helmet and putting it on afterwards" (*SI*, p. 136). This is one of those "great concepts" that Dickey says lie behind every great poem, but the poem is better in the idea than in the execution. Curiously, the concept itself is translated into a didacticism:

> On even the first day of death
> The dead cannot rise up,
> But their last thought hovers somewhere
> For whoever finds it.
>
> (*Poems*, p. 175)

6. Roethke, *The Collected Poems*, p. 60.

In Dickey's triumvirate of creative powers—will, abandon, and intellect—one sometimes dominates the other two. In this case, the intellect is supreme, and the result is a "thinky" poem lacking in spontaneity and emotional commitment. What could be worse than a bit of narrative transition like "Enough / Shining, I picked up my carbine and said"? And what could be more artificial than the description of the inherited last thought?

> I saw tremendous trees
> That would grow on the sun if they could,
> Towering. I saw a fence
> And two boys facing each other,
> Quietly talking,
> Looking in at the gigantic redwoods,
> The rings in the trunks turning slowly
> To raise up stupendous green.
> They went away, one turning
> The wheels of a blue bicycle,
> The smaller one curled catercornered
> In the handlebar basket.
>
> (*Poems*, p. 177)

With its cloyingly precious image of the little brother curled in the basket of big brother's bicycle, this scene has all the visionary power of a Norman Rockwell print. Even imagining that the passage suggests something of Dickey's own sense of longing for his dead older brother cannot save it.

"The Driver" is no more successful in its pursuit of communion with the dead, but it is more honest than "In the Tree House at Night" or "Drinking From a Helmet." In fact, it may be taken as a comment on why those efforts fail. From his position in the shattered driver's seat of a halftrack sunk in ten feet of water, the speaker tries to get used to "the burning stare / Of the wide-eyed dead after battle" (*Poems*, p. 169) by acting out in dangerous pantomime the role of the killed driver. Sitting there, with his lungs about to burst, he tries one last ploy to merge with the dead:

> "I become pure spirit," I tried
> To say, in a bright smoke of bubbles,

73

But I was becoming no more
Than haunted, for to be so
Is to sink out of sight, and to lose
The power of speech in the presence
Of the dead, with the eyes turning green.
                              (*Poems*, p. 170)

Significantly, it is language that fails, the incantatory assertion, "'I become pure spirit.'" But saying it and making it
so are two entirely different things, for to become pure
spirit the speaker would have to forego his last-second leap
to the surface and back into the world of the living.

Like the speaker in "The Driver," who wills a greater
sense of wholeness than he is prepared for or able to attain,
Dickey tries hard to sell himself on the idea of union with
the dead. Unfortunately, he never effects the merger and so
becomes "no more than haunted." Words, as powerful as
they are, are not enough to accomplish the feat. Consequently, "In the Tree House at Night" and "Drinking From
a Helmet" are little more than speculative formulations,
bubbles of words inadequate for the task at hand.

The problem, finally, is with language itself, which para-
doxically distances the poet from the very thing he wishes
to embrace. To verbalize at all is to end the dream of the
dog pursuing the fox, the vision of the fox fighting for its
life, and the sense of communion with the dead. The poem,
after all, is not the thing itself but only a representation or
an approximation, the product of the poet's aesthetic detachment. This dilemma is at the heart of one of Dickey's
best poems, "The Firebombing," and is expressed most
succinctly in the following lines:

It is this detachment,
The honored aesthetic evil,
The greatest sense of power in one's life,
That must be shed in bars, or by whatever
Means, by starvation
Visions in well-stocked pantries.
                              (*Poems*, p. 186)

Though it may seem strange to find an "aesthetic evil" at
the heart of a poem about a bomber pilot's inability to feel

guilt for his terrible actions during wartime, the pilot's sense of detachment is identical to the poet's. Both possess within them a frightening objectivity, a remoteness from things that enables them to observe and contemplate. Like the pilot who sails "artistically" over the land he is incinerating, sealed within his "pale treasure-hole of soft light / Deep in aesthetic contemplation" (*Poems*, p. 186), the poet drifts above his material. He can no more become the dead driver of a sunken halftrack than the pilot can change places with the people he killed. Through "visions in well-stocked pantries," some degree of empathy is possible, but the imagination can draw only so near to actual experience. Finally, both pilot and poet must admit to being "unable / To get down there or see / What really happened" (*Poems*, p. 188).

This is, of course, the ultimate failure of art. The created work is not life, though it may be lifelike, nor is it death, though it may be deathlike. Dickey succeeds most and attains the greatest credibility in those poems that acknowledge their own limitations. The speaker's claim at the end of "Drinking From a Helmet"—"I was the man"—sounds false because it is false. Though he may have projected himself through imagination into something like the identity of the dead soldier and intuited something like his last thought, he is not finally the dead soldier, for to be him is to be dead. The pilot in "The Firebombing," like the swimmer in "The Driver," may want to be more than merely haunted; but he, too, must come to the surface and choose life. Beneath him, the dead hold their silent screams as he breathes, accepting his inability to identify with them. Strangely, when Dickey acknowledges his failure, the dead seem more real in their separateness than in any proximity manufactured through false conjuring. And it is possible that some bond is established with the dead despite the failure, simply because an effort is made. This calls to mind the speaker's final hope in "Approaching Prayer." When considering what his drive toward vision has gained him, he concludes that more might have been accomplished than he was aware of: "That, if not heard, / It may have been somehow said" (*Poems,* p. 168). Knowing that the possibility for vision exists, that the words are being spoken despite his inability to hear them, is in itself a kind of vision.

It is in convincing us that we, too, can participate in such important failures that Dickey succeeds in selling God. The grand assertions of union with animals and with the dead are supported only by bravado and so present themselves less convincingly than the near misses. In his effort to perceive the wholeness of life, even when he fails or succeeds only for a fleeting moment, Dickey is entirely credible because it is the effort, after all, that is most important. For all his emphasis on daring and abandon, it is Dickey's humility before the singleness of the universe that finally makes his struggle worthy of our interest and even our participation. At his worst, in the character of the drunken Dutch poet of *The Zodiac,* Dickey is all bluster and swagger. His character is engaged in a solipsistic exercise, an attempt to define the universe in terms of himself, a process antithetical to Dickey's true approach. The way to a vision of wholeness is to will one's inclusion, not to impose oneself on the natural world. The idea is to become like the marsh grass rather than to make the marsh grass become like us.

V. AFTERWORD

In concluding the 1970 book *Self-Interviews*, Dickey made the following predictions about his future development as a poet: "I think I'll be moving more and more toward a narrative with less direct continuity than I've had before. I expect that this will inevitably result in my becoming more obscure than I have been. I want to work with extremely crazy, apparently unjustifiable juxtapositions and sudden shifts of meaning or consciousness." He went on in the same commentary to say, "If what I wish to do works out, I'll write even more discontinuous and undoubtedly more obscure poems, moving, I hope, eventually toward a greater clarity than I or anybody else has yet had" (*SI*, p. 185). There is something of Zen in his assertion, something reminiscent of the standard mystical precept—"The way down is the way up." If his contention sounds more like double-talk than a valid principle, it is because so many inferior writers have rationalized their failures using some version of the paradox. What further criticism can be launched against a poet who defends himself against charges of obscurity by saying, "Yes, I know; I intended to be obscure. Only through obscurity can I make you see"? Every young creative writer learns this strategy early, to claim weaknesses as strengths. But Dickey is no beginner, and so his use of the paradox must be taken as something more than the rationalization of laziness or failure.

Dickey's plans to become more obscure represent a premeditated defection from the central aesthetic of his poetry from 1960 to 1970: "a kind of plain-speaking line in which astonishing things could be said without rhetorical emphasis" (*Sorties*, p. 27). The movement away from a straightforward narrative style was not sudden and could be seen gaining momentum in poems like "May Day Sermon" and "Falling," which experiment with shifts and jumps of consciousness. These poems prepared the way for the manufactured craziness and often "unjustifiable juxtapositions" of *The Zodiac*, a poem in which Dickey gives himself license to do almost anything, no matter how foolish or unsupportable it may be.[1] After all, the Dutch poet's visions are not the product of poetic insight but of delirium tremens, and a drunken Dutch poet may think or say obscure and insane things. He may even imagine a lobster sign in the zodiac and then scream when it comes toward him with its claws readied to kill.

As different as it seems from Dickey's earlier work, *The Zodiac* does not represent an authentic change in direction. Because the book takes such an exaggerated stance, in the persona of the Dutch poet and in the length of his alcoholic maunderings, it proclaims itself a breakthrough of some kind, but it is essentially a tour de force of techniques previously exploited in such poems as "The Fiend" and "Mercy." The strategy is to get inside the consciousness of a character who is under some kind of pressure—mental, emotional, chemical—and then follow his unpredictable sprints of thought. Though *The Zodiac* is a departure from what Dickey has called the "anecdotal narratives" (*Motion*, p. v) characteristic of most of his work, the poem, for all its associational shifts, is still a narrative.

The true change in Dickey's poetry came with the publication of *Puella* in 1982, a book that looks all the more revolutionary alongside its immediate predecessor, *The Strength of Fields*. Published three years earlier, *The Strength of Fields* is basically a reprise or an encore performance of the kind of poetry that made Dickey's reputation in the 1960s. In fact, eight of the eleven poems constituting the first half of the book were originally published between 1969 and 1973. (The second half of the book is made up of improvised translations.) But *Puella* is entirely different

1. As Turner Cassity convincingly shows in an essay review titled "Double Dutch" (*Parnassus*, 8, no. 2 (1980): 177–93), Dickey also gave himself license to obscure the real source of *The Zodiac*. Although he claims to have based his poem broadly on Hendrick Marsman's poem of the same title, Dickey actually borrowed heavily from A. J. Barnou's translation of Marsman's original.

and represents, even for a poet who prizes and constantly struggles for change, a shift of revolutionary proportions. For Dickey personally, *Puella* offers not only a different kind of poetry but also a different poetics, a movement from an experience-oriented approach to one that is word oriented (*Night*, p. 313).

Dickey has valued change and experimentation, asserting that he would rather fail trying something new than to stagnate doing the same thing forever. While this attitude has made him exciting and provocative to read, it has occasionally made him outrageous and ridiculous as well. For the reader, of course, the element of danger implicit in Dickey's bold excursions makes him a poet worth following; and Dickey has played to that interest by choosing unexpected subjects for his poems and altering his style. The changes have satisfied both pitchman and artist, both Dickey's desire to sustain an interest in his work and an urge to explore new territory. But the changes made in *Puella* make such great demands on the reader that Dickey may lose a large part of his audience, for the reader is confronted not simply with a new subject or a new style but with a new Dickey.

A few contemporary poets have made significant changes in the kind of poetry they write; most notable among them are the two that Dickey himself has singled out, Theodore Roethke and Robert Lowell (*Night*, p. 321). But no recent poet other than Dickey has essayed so complete a revision of approach so late in his career. Far from whimsical, Dickey's change is a well thought out view of poetry best expressed in the following passage from Winfield Townley Scott's *Notebooks*, as quoted by Dickey in a paper of his own:

> There are two kinds of poetry. One, the kind represented by [Hart] Crane's line: "The seal's wide spindrift gaze toward paradise," the other represented by [Edward Arlington] Robinson's: "And he was all alone there when he died." One is a magic gesture of language, the other a commentary on human life so concentrated as to give off considerable pressure. The greatest poets combine the two; Shakespeare fre-

quently; Robinson himself now and then. If I have to choose, I choose the second: I go, in other words, for Wordsworth, for Hardy, in preference to Poe, to Rimbaud. . . . This is all an oversimplification, I know; but I think the flat assertion of the two kinds indicates two very great touchstones. (*Night*, p. 125)

However inadequate Scott's two divisions may be, Dickey emphatically declares them valid and useful. And though he identifies himself as one of the commentators on human life, he reveals a strong interest in the "magicians." Having spent a career writing the "plain-speaking line," creating "the clear pane of glass that does not call attention to itself, but gives clearly and cleanly on a circumstance" (*Night*, p. 126), Dickey has become attracted to the associational power of language, to words themselves as the point of focus. Assessing the change he has undertaken, Dickey says:

Recently I have tried, as the athletes say, to work out with the magical side of language: to break away from an approach that I felt was tending toward the anecdote, and depending too much upon it for whatever value this dependency might give it. Perhaps, in the latest poems I have done, this has been a mistake, but even if it has, I can still say that by the attempt I have been made aware of ranges of expression, of possibilities, of departures, of "new thresholds, new anatomies," that I previously had no idea existed, or certainly had no idea that I might explore. (*Night*, p. 133)

Curiously, Dickey has returned late in life to the dilemma he confronted at the outset of his career—whether lyric or narrative should dominate—and has decided to take the road not taken. The narrative element characteristic of most of his poetry becomes secondary to the lyrical power of language in the nineteen poems of *Puella*, which present a woman's "girlhood, male-imagined" (presumably the girlhood of Dickey's wife, Deborah), as the dedication indicates. The narrative task for Dickey is to project himself into the identity of a young girl and to imagine what moving from childhood into adulthood is like for her. Narratively, though, very little happens in *Puella*, as Dickey's fondness for story-line and action gives way to an exploration of Deborah's psychological and emotional transition to womanhood. Each poem is like a photograph in an album that is commanded to speak for itself: Deborah studying her face in a mirror; "Deborah in Ancient Lingerie"; Deborah "With Rose, at Cemetery"; Deborah at the piano. As a result, the poems have a static quality, as though they stand outside time, and language rather than action becomes the point of interest. Consider, for example, the opening passage from "Heraldic: Deborah and Horse in Morning Forest":

> It could be that nothing you could do
> Could keep you from stepping out and blooding-in
> An all-out blinding heraldry for this:
> A blurred momentum-flag
> That must be seen sleep-weathered and six-leggèd,
> Brindling and throwing off limbo-light.[2]

Swinburne would have been proud of such lines, filled as they are with an opulence of sounds—assonance, consonance, alliteration, internal rhymes, echo repetitions, and playful balances ("stepping out and blooding-in"). Hopkins, too, cited in an epigraph to the poem, would have found the language to his liking, particularly the compound "limbo-light" and the word "Brindling," which was probably Hopkins's in the first place ("a brinded cow"). Dickey is working the language for all the magic he can extract from it in the hope that his chosen words will create their own special reality. Moreover, his dependence on Hopkins, whom he holds up as one of the magicians, together with his repudiation of the supreme literalist Robinson, in an afterword to a 1981 reprinting of *Babel to Byzantium*, proclaims his new poetic direction.

With the poems of *Puella*, the pitchman has changed his product at some risk, for although Dickey would probably claim a special kind of "presentational immediacy" for these recent efforts, they lack the accessibility of most of

2. James Dickey, *Puella* (Garden City, N.Y.: Doubleday, 1982), p. 23. Cited hereafter as *Puella* in text.

his earlier work, including even *The Zodiac*. Knowing that change does not always signify growth, Dickey risks change for its own sake just to keep himself stimulated as a writer. As an element of personal artistic development, his attitude has merit, but his courageous pursuit of the new and different can easily lead in the wrong direction.

The ultimate question concerning Dickey's new venture is whether it is possible for a poet who belongs to one of the groups identified by Scott to change loyalties: can a self-avowed human life commentator transform himself into one of the magicians? Probably a poet belonging to either group finds himself a member not by choice but as a result of predisposition. One wonders how Robinson would have fared had he tried to write like Hart Crane, or how Crane would have done trying to be like Robinson. If Scott's method of classifying poets has any validity at all, it is by virtue of identifying two great kinds of poetic minds or talents, not alternatives that can be arbitrarily selected.

Dickey's decision to write a different kind of poetry is in part a product of his characteristic bravado. In his terms, he has decided "to work out with the magical side of language." His choice of metaphor suggests physical exertion, a determination to flex and develop muscles he has not been using very much, and recalls a passage from *Sorties* in which Dickey says he wants to be known as a writer with a "muscular sensibility" (*Sorties*, p. 63). Having proved he can bench-press the literalist approach, he now wants to show he can dead-lift the magical approach. That he gets the weight off the ground is in itself so remarkable that one hesitates to criticize his technique. The accomplishment, like Dickey's perceptions of wholeness, is the result of a remarkable power of the will; he should not be able to perform the feat at all.

To see how different the poetry in *Puella* is, one need only open at random one of Dickey's earlier books to find a contrasting example; the opening stanza of "The Hospital Window" will do:

> I have just come down from my father.
> Higher and higher he lies

implications about audience. Poems that are word oriented rather than experience oriented are more difficult to understand and therefore attract a smaller readership. Although Dickey may be hoping his readers will be willing to work harder to keep up with him, it is obvious that he is prepared to accept a smaller audience. This is a remarkable change in attitude for a writer who made his reputation by literally carrying his poetry across country to as many people as he could lure into an auditorium. Perhaps the pitchman has finally yielded to the poet. But given Dickey's temperament and his history, it is just as likely that the pitchman, sure of his abilities, intends to sell the new product as vigorously as he sold the old. One wonders if Dickey will continue to write in the *Puella* vein, and if he can gain a broad acceptance for his changed poetry.

While the pitchman may have been momentarily subdued in the poetry, he is as active as ever in other areas, busily preparing a third coffee-table book, this one on Appalachia, to go with his earlier successful ventures in this kind of commercialism, *Jericho: The South Beheld* and *God's Images*. In addition, Dickey published in 1983 a lengthy collection of essays, interviews, afterwords, and commencement addresses under the title *Night Hurdling*. Whether this volume will occasion as much negative criticism as its predecessors, *Self-Interviews* and *Sorties*, remains to be seen; it is similarly self-indulgent and self-promotional.

Of greatest significance, however, is a new volume of collected poems, *The Central Motion: Poems, 1968–1979*. As the title indicates, this collection is meant to take its place after *Poems 1957–1967* and before an as yet unpublished final collection. Interestingly, although the volume bears a 1983 copyright, it does not include the poems from *Puella*. Their omission suggests that Dickey, who seems obsessively concerned with organizing his poetic career for posterity, intends for the *Puella* poems to stand as the trumpet sound before the gate of a final and very different stage in his career. Just how conscious Dickey is of such niceties is best revealed by his manipulation of the dates for his middle collection. Although the title lists 1968–1979 as the timeframe, the book begins with selections from *The Eye-Beaters*, which was published in 1970. The discrepancy can be accounted for by the fact that some of the poems in that volume were published individually in 1968, but that does not explain why the volume itself is dated 1968 in Dickey's table of contents. Most likely, the date has been manipulated a little to mesh the book more smoothly with the earlier collection. Now we have a complete opus, in two volumes, stretching without gaps from 1957 through 1979. The pitchman behind the poet sees to it that even the smallest details of marketing are properly handled.

That Dickey has gained himself a seat in the pantheon of American poets is beyond dispute, but whether his will be a central throne or a folding chair off to the side must for the present remain obscure. It is clear, however, that Dickey has not been a nucleus of poetic activity. He has led no movements, has founded no schools, and has remained essentially independent. Consequently, his importance finally will be judged on the merits of his work alone rather than on the power of his influence or the strength of his literary connections. In this respect, he is in the excellent company of such originals as Dylan Thomas and Theodore Roethke, who also went their own ways; but individuality itself does not guarantee a position of prominence.

For the moment, Dickey's work is so closely tied to Dickey the man that it is impossible to hold the two far enough apart to render an objective assessment. Perhaps it will never be possible to do so. After all, Dickey has seen to it that his public persona will be transmitted to future readers along with his poetry, in the form of self-interviews, journals, and personal essays. This conflation may eventually prove to be Dickey's most unique contribution—his insistence on making himself as visible as his poetry, a decidedly postmodernist reaction to the modernist notion of authorial invisibility.

Though he is far from being confessional in his poetry, Dickey has certainly been so in his interviews and essays, carrying the confessionalist's interests in private revelations one step further to focus on his own artistic center.

He may be seen, then, as representing the most recent phase in a process that has moved logically from the poem as an objective artifact, to the poem as a subjective expression of the poet's thoughts and emotions, to a preoccupation with the process of creativity itself. In his poems, Dickey has little interest in disclosing his innermost personal thoughts; but in his commentaries he is obsessed with his own artistic ego and seems almost to view himself as a poetic specimen, probing and dissecting (with an enthusiastic curiosity many have found objectionable) to discover just what makes him go.

In the long run, Dickey's self-consciousness may come to be viewed more charitably as a strength, a courageous postmodernist stance, though it may just as possibly be perceived as weak self-absorption. Regardless of the final critical assessment, however, James Dickey will unquestionably be remembered as one who vigorously promoted himself and his work to gain whatever place he will eventually occupy among the poets of his time.